FIELD GUIDE TO

MICROSOFT
WINDOWS 95

PUBLISHED BY

Microsoft Press
A Division of Microsoft Corporation
One Microsoft Way
Redmond, Washington 98052-6399

Library of Congress Cataloging-in-Publication Data
Nelson, Stephen L., 1959-
  Field guide to Microsoft Windows 95 /Stephen L. Nelson.
    p.   cm.
  Includes index.
  ISBN 1-55615-675-8
  1. Operating systems (Computers)
  2. Microsoft Windows 95.
  I. Title.
QA76.76.063N444   1995
005.4'469--dc20   95-320
                                                   CIP

Printed and bound in the United States of America.

  2 3 4 5 6 7 8 9 BPress 9 8 7 6 5

Distributed to the book trade in Canada by Macmillan of
Canada, a division of Canada Publishing Corporation.

A CIP catalogue record for this book is available from the
British Library.

Microsoft Press books are available through
booksellers and distributors worldwide. For further
information about international editions, contact your local
Microsoft Corporation office. Or contact Microsoft Press
International directly at fax (206) 936-7329.

Macintosh and TrueType are registered trademarks of
Apple Computer, Inc. Genigraphics is a registered trade-
mark and GraphicsLink is a trademark of Genigraphics
Corporation. Harvard Graphics is a registered trademark
of Software Publishing Corporation. 1-2-3, Freelance
Graphics, and Lotus are registered trademarks of Lotus
Development Corporation. WordPerfect is a registered
trademark of WordPerfect Corporation.

Acquisitions Editor: Lucinda Rowley

Project Editor: John Pierce

Technical Contact: Mary DeJong

FIELD GUIDE TO

MICROSOFT
WINDOWS 95

Stephen L. Nelson

The Field Guide to Microsoft Windows 95 is divided into four sections. These sections are designed to help you find the information you need quickly.

1 ENVIRONMENT

Terms and ideas you'll want to know to get the most out of Windows 95. All the basic parts of Windows 95 are shown and explained. The emphasis here is on quick answers, but most topics are cross-referenced so that you can find out more if you want to.

Diagrams of key Windows 95 components, with quick definitions, cross-referenced to more complete information.

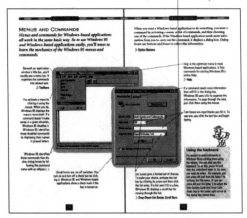

Tipmeister

Watch for me as you use this Field Guide. I'll point out helpful hints and let you know what to watch for.

17 WINDOWS 95 A TO Z

An alphabetic list of commands, tasks, terms, and procedures.

Definitions of key concepts and terms, and examples showing you why you should know them.

Quick identification of tools.

Step-by-step guides to performing most Windows 95 tasks.

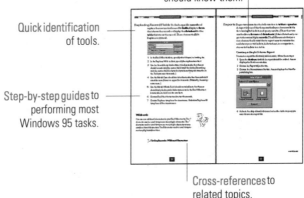

Cross-references to related topics.

147 TROUBLESHOOTING

A guide to common problems—how to avoid them and what to do when they occur.

167 QUICK REFERENCE

Useful indexes, including a full list of menu commands, shortcut keys, and more.

175 INDEX

A complete reference to all elements of the Field Guide.

INTRODUCTION

•••

In the field and on expedition, you need practical solutions. Fast. This Field Guide provides just these sorts of lightning quick answers. But take two minutes and read the Introduction. It explains how this unusual little book works.

WHAT IS A FIELD GUIDE?

Sometime during grade school, my parents gave me a field guide to North American birds. With its visual approach, its maps, and its numerous illustrations, that guide delivered hours of enjoyment. The book also helped me better understand and more fully appreciate the birds in my neighborhood. And the small book fit neatly in a child's rucksack. But I'm getting off the track.

This book works in the same way as that field guide to North American birds. It organizes information visually with numerous illustrations. And it does this in a way that helps you more easily understand and, yes, even enjoy working with Microsoft Windows 95. For new users, the Field Guide provides a visual path to the essential information necessary to start using Windows 95. But this Field Guide isn't only for beginners. For experienced users, it provides concise, easy-to-find descriptions of Windows 95 tasks, terms, and techniques.

HOW TO USE THIS BOOK

Let me explain how to find the information you need. You'll usually want to start by flipping to the first section, Environment, which is really a visual index. There you'll find the picture that shows what you want to do or the task you have a question about. For example, if you want to work with some thingamajig in a dialog box, you flip to pages 12 and 13, which show a dialog box.

Next you read the captions that describe the parts of the picture—or key elements of Windows 95. Say, for example, that you can't figure out how to use a dialog box button. The dialog box shown on pages 12 and 13 includes captions that describe the parts of a dialog box. These key elements appear in **boldface** type to make them stand out.

You'll notice that some captions are followed by little paw prints and additional **boldface** terms. These refer to entries in the second section, Windows 95 A to Z, which provide more information related to the caption's contents. (The paw prints show you how to track down the information you need. Get it?)

Windows 95 A to Z is a dictionary of more than 200 entries that define terms and describe tasks. (After you've worked with Windows 95 a bit or if you're already an experienced user, you'll often be able to turn directly to this section.) So, for example, if you have just read the caption that says Windows 95 provides online **Help**, you can flip to the "Help" entry in Windows 95 A to Z.

Any time an entry in Windows 95 A to Z appears as a term within an entry, I **boldface** it the first time it appears in the entry. For example, as part of describing how Help works, I might tell you that Help is a separate **application**. In this case, the word **application** appears in boldface letters to let you know that Windows 95 A to Z includes an entry called "Application." If you don't understand the term or want to do a bit of brushing up, you can flip to that entry for more information.

The third section, Troubleshooting, describes problems that new or casual users of Windows 95 often encounter. Following each problem description, I list one or more solutions that you can employ to fix the problem.

The Quick Reference describes the Start menu, Windows Explorer, My Computer, and the Printers menu **commands**. If you want to know what a specific command does, turn to the Quick Reference. Don't forget about the Index, either. You can look there to find all references in this book to any single topic.

CONVENTIONS USED HERE

I have developed two other conventions to make using this book easier for you. Rather than use wordy phrases, such as "Activate the File menu and then choose the Print command," to describe how you choose a command, I simply say "Choose the File Print command."

And to describe how you find and start applications or find and open documents using the **Start menu,** I tell you to click the **Start button,** and then I list in order the menu items you click next. For example, I might say "Click the Start button, and then choose Programs, Accessories, System Tools, and Backup." I think this approach works much better than the more wordy alternative, "Click the Start button. Then choose Programs in the Start menu, choose Accessories in the Programs **submenu,** choose System Tools in the Accessories submenu, and, finally, choose Backup in the System Tools submenu." Whew.

ENVIRONMENT

Need to get the lay of the land quickly? Then the Environment is the place to start. It defines the key terms you'll need to know and the core ideas you should understand as you begin exploring Windows 95.

THE WINDOWS 95 DESKTOP

Turning on your computer starts Microsoft Windows 95.
When Windows 95 starts, you see the Windows 95 desktop.

This is the Windows 95 desktop.

This is the My Computer icon. Double-click it to see a picture of your computer's disks, printers, and Control Panel tools.

This is the Network Neighborhood icon. Double-click it to see a picture of the network you're connected to.

This is the Start button. I'll talk more about how you use this button on pages 4 & 5.
❖ Opening Files; Starting Windows-Based Applications

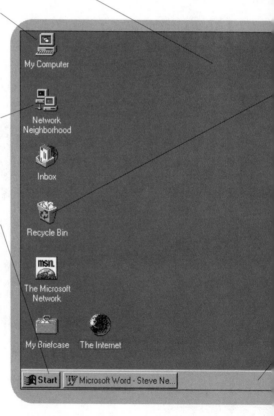

My Computer

Network Neighborhood

Inbox

Recycle Bin

msn.
The Microsoft Network

My Briefcase   The Internet

Start   Microsoft Word - Steve Ne..

You'll want to learn the names of the parts of the desktop. Learning the names will make your introduction to Windows 95 easier. And it will ensure that we (you and I) use a common vocabulary in the pages that follow.

This is the Recycle Bin icon. Double-click it to see the Recycle Bin folder, a container that holds recently deleted files.

※ Folder; Recycle Bin

This is the Taskbar. I'll talk more about how you use this tool on pages 6 & 7.

Logging on

Windows 95, as it starts, asks you for a user name and password. If your computer connects to a network, Windows 95 uses this information to log you on to the network.

STARTING APPLICATIONS

Typically, you start applications by clicking the Start button, choosing Programs, and then choosing an application name either from the Programs menu or from one of its submenus.

Shortcut icons are miniature pictures that represent documents you want to open quickly and often. To open the document represented by a shortcut icon, just double-click it.

The Start menu organizes your **applications** and recently used **documents**. It also includes **commands** for **exiting Windows 95** and for changing the way your computer operates.
❖ **Control Panel; Help**

Click the Start button to start **applications** and open files.
❖ **Opening Files; Starting Windows-Based Applications**

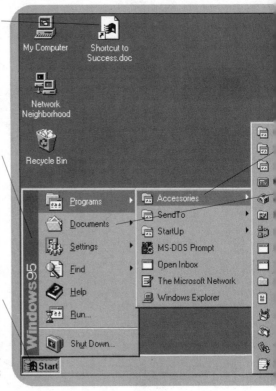

4

To display the items listed on a submenu, you move the mouse so its on-screen pointer rests over the submenu you want to select.

To choose an item from a menu, you move the mouse so that its on-screen pointer rests over the item you want to select. Then you **click** the mouse's left button.

You can also start an application by telling Windows 95 you want to open a **document**—such as a letter or a report you're writing. When you tell Windows 95 to open a document, Windows 95 first starts the application that created the document. Then it tells that application to open the document.

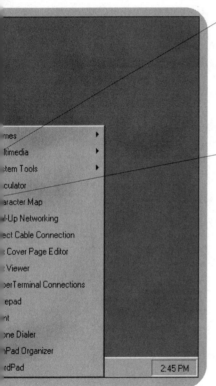

mes
ltimedia
stem Tools
culator
aracter Map
al-Up Networking
ect Cable Connection
Cover Page Editor
Viewer
perTerminal Connections
epad
nt
ne Dialer
Pad Organizer
rdPad   2:45 PM

Applications appear either on the **Programs menu** or on one of its **submenus,** such as the **Accessories** menu. Items on the Start menu that display a submenu of additional items show a triangle.
❖ **Folder**

The Documents submenu displays the most recently used 15 **documents,** or **files.** To simultaneously start an application and have it open one of these documents, just choose a document from this menu.
❖ **Start Menu**

Using the StartUp menu

Windows 95 automatically starts applications listed on the StartUp menu. If you always start an application when you start Windows 95, add the application to the StartUp menu.

❖ **Starting Windows-Based Applications**

RUNNING MULTIPLE APPLICATIONS

Windows 95 allows you to run several applications at once so that you can work more quickly and share information more easily.

The foreground application displays its **application window** in front of the other application windows. Your **commands, clicks,** and keystrokes usually affect the foreground application.

Multitasking just means you can start and then run more than one application at a time. Windows 95 allows you to multitask.

Once started, an application appears in its own window, called an **application window**.

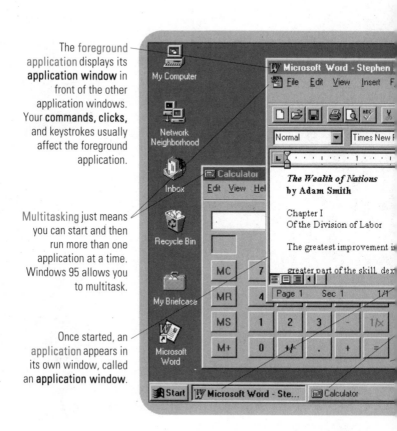

To run multiple **applications,** you just start more than one. (Until you exit from an application, it keeps running.) Windows 95 displays each application in its own window.

One of the running applications is called the **foreground application** because its window appears in front of all the others and because it's the one your **commands** affect. You can easily move a **background application** to the foreground by **clicking** its **application window** or its **Taskbar** button.

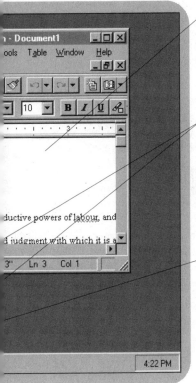

Applications that open documents display windows that are called **document windows.**

The Taskbar shows buttons for any applications you've started. To switch between applications you've started, click the buttons shown on the Taskbar.

❖ Switching Tasks

Background applications display their application windows behind the foreground application window. A background application is still running. But to issue a command to one, you typically need to first move it to the foreground.

WINDOWS 95 SYSTEM TOOLS

Windows 95 lets you view visual maps that represent your computer system, and it includes tools for managing devices like printers, disks, and modems.

My Computer displays a graphical map of your computer, including its disks and any **printers** you've connected to the computer.

Network Neighborhood displays a similar graphical map of the network to which your computer is connected. Just double-click the icon to see the map.

Windows 95 identifies the disk drives, both the **floppy disks** and **hard disks**, connected to your computer by using **icons.** If you want to see which **folders** and **files** are on a disk, double-click the disk's icon.

The Printers folder shows the printers you've added to your computer system and any documents you're **printing.** It also includes a **wizard** for adding new printers.

☞ Print Queue

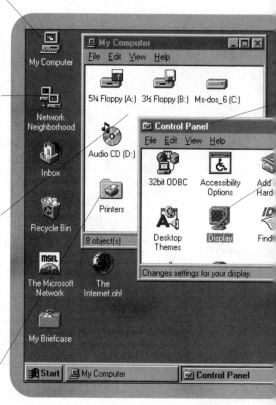

Windows 95 displays a graphical map of your computer called My Computer. You can tell Windows 95 to display the My Computer map in a window by double-clicking the My Computer icon. You can also display a similar map of the network your computer connects to (if it does connect) by double-clicking the Network Neighborhood icon.

Control Panel includes nearly two dozen tools for changing **properties,** or the way your computer works. You can change the colors your desktop shows, for example, using the Display tool.

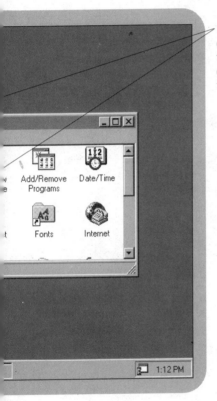

The System Tools folder

Windows 95 also provides a System Tools folder that holds helpful disk management tools for **backing up, defragmenting,** and compressing your disks with **DriveSpace.**

9

WINDOW MANAGEMENT

You can manage application and document windows by clicking buttons that appear around the edges of the window, by using the Control menu commands, or by dragging the window border.

Click the Control menu icon to display a menu of commands for managing a window. A Control menu icon appears in the upper left corner of both application windows and document windows.

☙ **Control Menu Commands**

Title bars identify the **application** displayed in a window and, usually, any **documents** displayed in a **document window**. The title bars for the active application window and active document window show in different colors than do the title bars for the inactive application window and inactive document window.

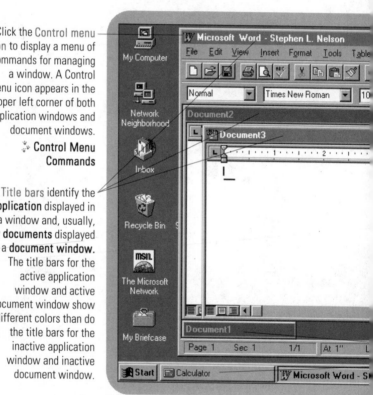

All windows can be moved and resized. You can, for example, expand an application window so that it fills the screen and expand a document window so that it fills the application window displaying it. If an application window displays document windows, you can also move and resize these as well as activate one document window so that it appears at the top of the stack.

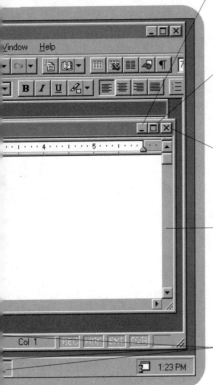

Click the Minimize button to shrink a window so that the window appears only as a button at the bottom of the screen.
⁂ **Window Buttons**

Click the Maximize/Restore button to maximize the window or, if the window is already maximized, to undo the previous Maximize Window command.

Click the Close button to close the window. Closing an **application window** stops the **application**.
⁂ **Exiting Windows-Based Applications**

Scroll bars let you page through a document when its contents won't fit in the window. Windows 95 provides horizontal and vertical scroll bars. Usually, you can also use the PgUp and PgDn keys to move up and down in a window.
⁂ **Scrolling**

Minimized windows appear as buttons near the bottom edge of the screen. Minimized application windows appear as buttons on the **Taskbar**. Minimized document windows appear in a row along the bottom edge of the application window.

MENUS AND COMMANDS

Menus and commands for Windows-based applications all work in the same basic way. So to use Windows 95 and Windows-based applications easily, you'll want to learn the mechanics of the Windows 95 menus and commands.

Beneath an application window's title bar, you'll usually see a menu bar. It organizes the commands into related sets.

⁂ Toolbars

You activate a menu by clicking it using the mouse. When you do, Windows 95 displays the menu's commands. If a command doesn't make sense in a given situation, Windows 95 disables it. Windows 95 identifies these disabled commands by displaying their names in grayed letters.

Windows 95 identifies those commands that display dialog boxes by following the command name with an ellipsis (...).

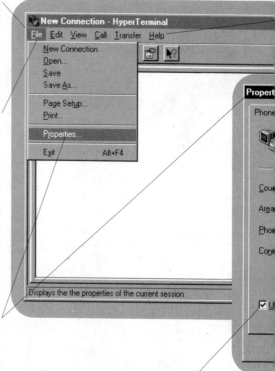

Check boxes are on-off switches. You turn on and turn off a check box by clicking it. Windows 95 and Windows-based applications show a check mark if the box is turned on.

When you want a Windows-based application to do something, you issue a command by activating a menu, or list of commands, and then choosing one of the commands. If the Windows-based application needs more information from you to carry out the command, it displays a dialog box. Dialog boxes use buttons and boxes to collect this information.

Option Buttons

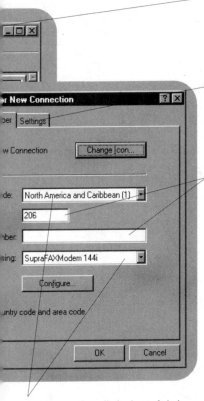

Help is the rightmost menu in most Windows-based applications. It lists commands for starting Windows 95's online Help.

Help

If a command needs more information than will fit in the dialog box, Windows 95 uses tabs to organize the information. To page through the tabs, just click them using the mouse.

Text boxes are input blanks you fill in. To use one, you click the text box and begin typing.

Using the keyboard

It's easiest to select elements in Windows 95 by clicking them using the mouse. You can also use the keyboard. To do this, press Alt and then the underlined letter in the item you want to select. For example, you can press Alt and then the letter F to activate the File menu. Or you can press Alt and the letter U to select the Use Country Code And Area Code check box in the lower right corner of the dialog box shown here.

List boxes give a limited set of choices. To make your choice, activate the list box by clicking its arrow and then click the list entry. If a list won't fit in a box, Windows 95 displays a scroll bar for moving through the list.

Drop-Down List Boxes; Scroll Bars

WINDOWS EXPLORER

Windows Explorer lets you look at the way your computer system is organized and at the stuff you've got connected to your computer.

Folders organize the contents of a disk. Folders also organize your printers, fonts, and the contents of the Recycle Bin. To see the **files** and **subfolders** in a **folder,** click the folder icon.

The folder pane shows the disks and folders on your computer.

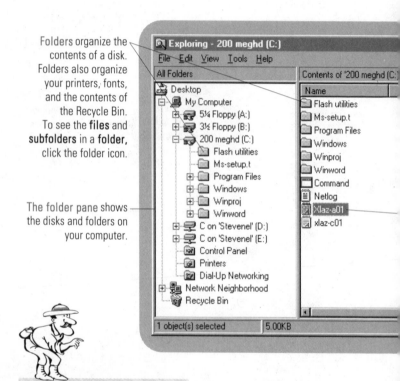

A little history lesson, Part I

Folders, as you might have already guessed, essentially replace MS-DOS's directories. Note, however, that Windows 95 uses folders to organize things besides the files on a disk. Folders are also used to organize Control Panel tools, printers, and fonts.

You don't need to use Windows Explorer. But if you're more than a casual computer user, you'll find it invaluable for working with your disks and files. You can copy and move files and folders by clicking and dragging the mouse, for example. You can also rename files and folders by clicking and typing. And you can easily delete (and often undelete) files and folders and format disks by choosing menu commands.

⁂ Copying Files; Erasing Files; File Names; Recycle Bin

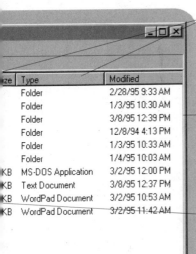

File pane buttons let you sort and re-sort the folder's contents by name, size, type, and date last modified. If the file pane buttons don't appear, choose the View Details command to see them.

The file pane shows the subfolders and files in the selected folder. Windows 95 uses different icons to help identify folders and the types of files.

⁂ Formatting Floppy Disks

Select files and folders by clicking them using the mouse or by using the Tab and arrow keys.

⁂ Copying Files, Erasing Files, File Names, Moving Files, Recycle Bin

A little history lesson, Part II

Windows Explorer replaces Program Manager and File Manager, which were available in earlier versions of Windows. If you still want to use either of these applications, you can. You start them in the same way you start other Windows-based applications.

WINDOWS 95 A TO Z

Maybe it's not a jungle out there. But you'll still want to keep a survival kit close at hand. Windows 95 A to Z, which starts on the next page, is just such a survival kit. It lists in alphabetic order the tools, terms, and techniques you'll need to know.

16-Bit MS-DOS was a 16-bit operating system and moved data around in chunks that look like this:

0101110010011001

Ten years ago or so, this was fine. Everybody was happy. But then we all got greedy. We—or at least some of us—wanted more power. No, that's not quite right. We *needed* more power.

Unfortunately, a 16-bit operating system limited us in a couple of ways. For example, it moved chunks of data that were needlessly small because the newest personal computer processors handle data in **32-bit** chunks. These bigger chunks look like this:

0101110010011001010111001001100

But there was another problem with the 16-bit operating system. It required software developers to do all sorts of crazy things if they wanted to work with large amounts of **memory** and disk space.

Earlier versions of Microsoft Windows, by the way, were mostly 16-bit software. Windows 95, in comparison, is mostly 32-bit software.

32-Bit Windows 95 is a 32-bit operating system. This provides a couple of neat benefits. First, it's faster because you're moving chunks of data around that are twice as big as they would be in a **16-bit** operating system. Second, it lets you access monstrously large amounts of **memory** and disk space. (Windows 95 can work with as much as 4 **gigabytes** of memory and with disks as large as 137 gigabytes.)

Since we're on the subject of 32-bit operating systems, I should probably tell you that Windows 95, unlike Windows NT, isn't totally a 32-bit operating system. Some parts of the operating system are still 16-bit so that it will be compatible with your old **applications** and will run smoothly with a minimum amount of memory (4 MB).

Accessories
Windows 95 comes with a bunch of mini-**applications** like **Calculator** and **WordPad.** (Some call these babies "accessories.") Windows 95 stores them in the Accessories **folder.**

Active and Inactive Windows
The active **application window**—such as the Microsoft Word application window—is the one that appears in front of all other application windows. (Cleverly, this is called the "foreground." The inactive application windows, if there are inactive applications, appear in what's called the "background.")

The active **document window** is the one that appears in front of all other document windows in the application window. Any commands you choose affect the document in the active document window.

Activating Application Windows
You can activate a different application window either by clicking the application window's button on the **Taskbar** or by clicking the window if it's visible. You can also cycle through all the open application windows by pressing Alt+Tab.

Activating Document Windows
You can activate a different document window either by clicking the window or by choosing the Window menu command that names the window.

Active Document

The active document is the one that appears in front of any other **documents** in an **application window.** It's also the document that selected commands act on.

In a word processor **application,** you'll see whatever it is you're writing—a report, for example—in a document window. In a spreadsheet application, you'll see the spreadsheet you're creating in a document window. Many applications—perhaps most of them—let you display more than one document window in the application window.

Changing the Active Document

You can flip-flop between open documents—if you've got more than one open—by choosing one of the numbered menu commands on the Window menu. Each numbered command names an open document window. You can also press Ctrl+F6 to move to the next document window.

Animation

Animation just means movement. I mention this because Windows 95 uses lots of animation. Sure, some of the animation is probably gratuitous. But much of it isn't. It can help users—particularly new users—understand how Windows 95 works and what Windows 95 is currently doing.

Here is some of the animation you'll see if you keep your eyes peeled: There's a moving "pointing arrow with message" that points to the **Start button** and instructs you to click there to start Windows-based **applications.** (Purely instructive.) When you open a **folder** using **Windows Explorer,** the folder expands and opens to show its contents. (Again, purely instructive.) Then there's the Copying Files **message box** with its flying document **icons.** (OK, gratuitous.)

ANSI Characters The ANSI character set includes all the ASCII characters your keyboard shows plus the special characters your keyboard doesn't show, such as the Japanese yen symbol (¥) or the British pound symbol (£). Even though these special characters don't appear on your keyboard, you can still use them in most Windows-based **applications.** For example, you can enter ANSI characters in word processor **documents** or enter an ANSI character in most **text boxes.** To do all this, you use the **Character Map** application.

Antiques Some of the **applications** you may have used in earlier versions of Windows are obsolete in Windows 95. The old **Write** application has been replaced with **WordPad.** And Program Manager and File Manager have been replaced with **Windows Explorer.**

You can still use any of these old applications; however, you'll need to start them using Windows Explorer.

> ⁖ **Troubleshooting: You Want to Use a 3.0, 3.1, or 3.11 Application**

Application Applications are the programs that come with your computer or that you buy down at the software store or through the mail to do such work as word processing, accounting, and creating spreadsheets and databases.

Microsoft sells several well-known and popular applications, including Microsoft Word (a word processor application), Microsoft Excel (a spreadsheet application), and Microsoft Access (a database application). There are lots of other popular and well-known applications; WordPerfect, Lotus 1-2-3, and Quicken are just three of them. In this book, by the way, I'll always refer to these software programs as "applications."

> ⁖ **Exiting Windows-Based Applications; Starting Windows-Based Applications**

Application Errors
Sometimes an **application** asks Windows 95 to do the impossible. When this happens, Windows 95 displays a **message box** that alerts you to an application error.

∴ **Troubleshooting: You Get an Application Error**

Application Window
The application window is the rectangle in which an **application** such as Lotus 1-2-3, Microsoft Excel, Microsoft Word, or WordPerfect displays its **menu bars**, **toolbars**, and any open **document windows.**

ASCII Text Files
An ASCII text file is simply a **file** that uses only the characters your keyboard shows. You can usually import an ASCII text file into a spreadsheet or word processor **application** using the application's File Open command.

Sharing Data Among Applications
A last-resort method for sharing data among applications is to create an ASCII text file. This works because many applications—spreadsheet, database, and accounting applications, among others—produce text files.

∴ **Copying Data; Moving Data; Opening Files**

Background Applications
Windows 95 lets you run more than one **application** at a time. One of your applications runs in the foreground, meaning that it is the application that your commands affect and the application that has the most visible or the only visible window.

The other applications run in the background. Often, background applications' windows are not visible. You can't issue commands to a background application unless you first make it active or move it to the foreground.

People sometimes refer to background applications as "inactive applications" because they appear in what Windows 95 terms "inactive windows." This is an inaccurate description, however. A so-called "inactive application" is still working.

Background application messages

When a background application wants to display a message, its **title bar** or **Taskbar** button may flash, alerting you to the message. Microsoft Excel, for example, includes an AutoSave feature that prompts you via a **message box** to save the open file every so often. If you've moved Excel to the background, it can't display the message that asks about the AutoSave. So Excel flashes its application window title bar or Taskbar button.

➤ **Foreground Applications; Switching Tasks**

Backing Up An easy way to back up (make a copy of) a single **file** or even a handful of **folders** and files is to copy them to a **floppy disk.** If you want to make things easier and you've got a handful of small folders and files that can fit on a floppy disk or two, you may be able to use the Microsoft Backup **application.**

Starting Backup

To start Backup, click the **Start button.** Then choose Programs, Accessories, System Tools, and Backup. Windows 95 displays an introduction dialog box. It gives you the lay of the land. Click OK to continue. Backup displays a window that shows another dialog box. Click OK again.

continues

Backing Up *(continued)*

Running a Backup

Your first step in backing up is to identify the folders and files you want to back up. You do this using the Microsoft Backup window's Backup **tab**.

1   Select the folders and files you want to back up by clicking them. Backup marks selected folders and files with a checkmark.

2   Click Next Step. Backup displays a new set of options that asks which destination you want to use to back up the folders and files.

3   Select the destination you want to use to back up.

4   Click Start Backup. Backup displays a simple dialog box that asks you to name the Backup Set. (This set is the set of folders and files you are backing up.)

5   Name the Backup Set. Go on. Do it.

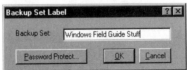

6   Click OK to start copying the folders and files. When Backup finishes, it displays a message box telling you so. Click OK to remove
this message. Click OK again to remove the Backup dialog box,
which describes the progress of the backup.

Restoring from a Backup Set

To restore a set of folders and files you've backed up, start Backup (as
described earlier), click the Restore tab, and insert the floppy disk or
tape cartridge that holds the backup set. Then follow these steps.

1   Select the destination you'll restore from.

2   Select the backup set.

3   Click Next Step. Backup displays a new set of options that names
the folders and files in the backup set and asks you which ones
should be restored.

4   Select the folders and files you want to restore by clicking them.

5   Click Start Restore. Backup restores the folders and files. When it
finishes, it displays message boxes telling you the restore is complete. Click OK a couple of times.

Battery Meter If you're using a **laptop computer,** Windows 95 displays a battery meter at the right end of the **Taskbar.** If you're running your laptop computer from the battery, this battery meter shows a picture of a battery. You can tell roughly how much juice you've got left by looking at how full the battery is. If the battery in the picture is only half full, you've used up half the battery's capacity.

If you're running your laptop computer from an electrical outlet, the battery meter shows a picture of a power cord plug.

Bit Map A bit map is simply a pattern of colored dots. On your screen, each colored dot is created as a pixel of light and is described by one or more bits (binary digits). This sounds like a bunch of gobbledygook, but if the pattern arranges the colored dots in the right way, you get a picture.

As a point of historical reference, I'll also mention that probably the best-known bit maps were those created in the late nineteenth century by the French impressionist painter Seurat. In this case, however, the colored dots were created by brushstrokes on canvas rather than by pixels of light. And you thought this book was just about computers.

Booting Using MS-DOS

Here's a little-known secret about Windows 95. It comes with a new version of **MS-DOS.** That's weird, right? You may want to know about this new version of MS-DOS, however, because you can use it in place of Windows 95. In other words, even though you've installed Windows 95 and have forgotten all about MS-DOS, you can still start, or boot, your computer using this new version of MS-DOS.

To boot your computer using MS-DOS, press the F8 function key when you see the message, "Starting Windows 95." This message appears shortly after you turn on your computer or after you reboot your computer by pressing Ctrl+Alt+Del. Windows 95 displays the Microsoft Windows 95 Startup menu, which lists as many as 8 startup options. By selecting the Command Prompt Only option, you tell Windows 95 not to load itself but instead to start MS-DOS. The next thing you know, you see the familiar MS-DOS prompt. If you then want to use an MS-DOS **application,** you can do so in the usual way.

So why would you do this? Good question. In many ways, running MS-DOS applications under, or from inside of, Windows 95 is best. I'm not going to go into all of the gory details here, but Windows 95 allows you to set up **virtual machines** for each of the MS-DOS applications you want to run. Technical gurus think this is really neat. But it may still be that you don't want to run MS-DOS applications under Windows 95 for this simple reason: They may not work right.

Briefcase   The Briefcase **application** lets you work with the same **file,** or **document,** on more than one computer—but without having to worry about whether you're working with the most current version. This may sound like no big deal, but here's an example that shows otherwise. Let's say that you've absolutely got to finish writing a report within a week. Perhaps your boss is on your back—nagging, whining, complaining; well, you know what I mean. So you've been working a bit on the report at the office. But some nights you've been taking the file home, on a **floppy disk,** to work with it on your **laptop computer.** After about three days of this, I promise, you'll have about half a dozen versions of the report file. And with a little bad luck, none of the versions will contain all your information and all your changes. This, my friend, is the problem Briefcase prevents. You can store a file in a briefcase and then use and carry around the briefcase. Windows 95 automatically keeps track of the files in your briefcase.

Creating a Briefcase

Windows 95 may have already created a briefcase for you, as part of its setup. If that's the case, you'll see the My Briefcase **icon** on your desktop.

This is the My Briefcase icon.

My Briefcase

If you don't see the My Briefcase icon on the desktop, you can create one. Click the **Start button.** Then choose Settings and Control Panel. When Windows 95 displays the Control Panel window, double-click the Add/Remove Programs icon. Next, when Windows 95 displays the Add/Remove Programs Properties dialog box, click the Windows Setup tab, click the Accessories entry in the list box, click the Details command button, click the Briefcase check box, and click OK.

Adding Files to a Briefcase

You add files to a briefcase by copying them. You **copy files** to a briefcase in the same way that you copy them to a **folder**.

Moving a Briefcase to a Floppy Disk

You move a briefcase to a floppy disk—so that you can use the floppy disk on your laptop for example—by moving it to the floppy disk icon. You do this by starting **Windows Explorer** and then dragging the My Briefcase icon to the floppy disk icon. When you move your briefcase, all the files it contains are copied to the floppy disk.

To use files in your briefcase on another computer, just stick the floppy disk that holds the briefcase into the other computer's floppy disk drive, and then open the files stored on the floppy disk.

Synchronizing Briefcase Files

After you've worked with the files a bit on the second computer, you'll want to update the files on the first computer. To do this, insert the floppy disk in the first computer's floppy disk drive. Then move your briefcase back to the first computer's desktop by dragging it from the floppy disk. To update the briefcase files, double-click the My Briefcase icon. When Windows 95 displays the My Briefcase window, select the files you want to update, and then choose either the Briefcase Update All or Briefcase Update Selection command.

Byte ⁘ Kilobyte

Calculator Use the Calculator **application** to make quick calculations.

Starting Calculator

Start Calculator by clicking the **Start button.** Then choose Programs, Accessories, and Calculator.

Using Calculator

Calculator in Windows 95 works pretty much like a regular, hand-held calculator.

If you've got a mouse, you can click the calculator keys to enter the numbers and the operators.

The calculator keys work like command buttons. Here are some sample calculations:

Buttons you click	Result
3-2=	1
1+1=	2
5-2=	3
2*2=	4
10/2=	5
36sqrt	6

Clearing and Erasing Calculator Inputs

You use the C key to clear the numbers and operators you entered, the CE key to clear the last number you entered, and the Back key to clear the last digit you entered. For example, if you've just entered 10+25, here's what the C, CE, and Back keys do:

Key	What it does
C	Clears all the numbers and operators you typed—in this case, 10+25
CE	Clears only the last number you typed—in this case, 25
Back	Clears only the last digit you typed—in this case, 5

Using the Percent Key

The calculator's percent (%) key lets you add, subtract, divide, and multiply a number by a percent. Here are some sample calculations:

If you click	Result	And what happens
10+50%=	15	Adds 50% of the value 10 to 10
10-50%=	5	Subtracts 50% of the value 10 from 10
10*50%=	50	Multiplies the value 10 by 50% of the value 10
10/50%=	2	Divides the value 10 by 50% of the value 10

Using the Inverse Key

The calculator's 1/x, or inverse, key divides 1 by the entered value. For example, if you enter 7 1/x=, Calculator returns 0.1428571428571 because 1/7 equals 0.1428571428571. If you click 1/x while this value shows on the calculator display, Calculator returns 7 because 1/0.1428571428571 equals 7.

continues

Calculator *(continued)*

Working with Memory

Calculator includes a memory feature, too. Click the MS key to store the displayed value in memory. When you do, Calculator displays the letter "M" in the box beneath the calculator display. Click M+ to add the displayed value to whatever is already stored in memory. Click MC to clear the value stored in memory. Click MR to retrieve the value stored in memory.

Copying and Pasting Values

Calculator's Edit Copy and Edit Paste commands let you move values to and from the **Clipboard.** Choose Edit Copy to place the value on the calculator display on the Clipboard. Choose Edit Paste to move the value on the Clipboard to the calculator display. Note that you can use the Edit Copy and Edit Paste commands to move values from Calculator to other Windows-based applications.

Using the Scientific Calculator

Calculator's View menu displays two commands: Scientific and Standard. They let you switch between the calculator shown earlier and a special version of the calculator that has keys for performing mathematical, trigonometric, and logarithmic operations.

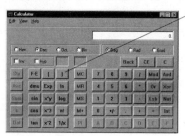

Use the parenthesis keys to perform calculations in some order other than the order in which you enter the operators.

CD Player Windows 95 comes with an **application** called CD Player that you can use to listen to music while you're working with your computer (if you have speakers and a CD-ROM drive). Or you can use it to listen to music while you're playing with your computer. As I'm writing this, for example, I'm listening to Pearl Jam. And, yes, this probably does impair my productivity.

Playing Music

To play a CD using CD Player, follow these steps:

1 Load a CD into your CD-ROM drive. If this is the first time you've done this, you may want to start with something mellow: Tony Bennett. Bach. Def Leppard.

2 Adjust the speaker volumes. Or if you use a headphone set, gently put it on.

3 Enjoy.

Easy listening

If you've just read the preceding steps and are thinking, "Hey, he never told me to start the CD Player application," you're right. But here's the deal. You don't have to start CD Player. Windows 95 figures that if you've just stuck, say, Sinatra into your CD player, you've done so because you want to hear the Chairman of the Board sing. Neat, huh? Some people call this "spin and grin." Windows 95 calls it "AutoPlay."

You *can* start the CD Player application yourself, if you want to. To do this, click the **Start button**. Then choose Programs, Accessories, Multimedia, and CD Player.

continues

CD Player (continued)

Fiddle-Faddling with CD Player

Once Windows 95 or you start CD Player, you can use it to replay favorite tracks, skip the ones you don't like, and do all the same sorts of things you might do with a regular, home stereo CD player.

To switch to the CD Player application, click its button on the **Taskbar**. Windows 95 then displays the CD Player application window.

Click this button to start the music.

Click this button to stop the music.

Click these buttons to move to the next and previous tracks.

Character Map The Character Map **application** lets you easily add characters that don't appear on your keyboard to **documents.** For example, if you want to add one of the following Wingdings characters, or symbols, to a document, the easiest and only practical way to do so is to use Character Map.

Starting Character Map

To start Character Map, click the **Start button.** Then choose Programs, Accessories, and Character Map. If you can't find Character Map, you'll need to install it using the Control Panel's Add/Remove Program tool.

Using Character Map

To use Character Map, follow these steps.

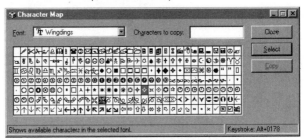

1 Activate the Font drop-down list box, and select the **font** that includes the character you want. (If you want to enlarge the symbol after you add it, you'll find that scalable fonts such as **TrueType** or **PostScript** work best.)

2 Find the character you want. If you can't see the characters very well—and I never can—click each character box and hold down the mouse button. Character Map displays a **pop-up box** showing an enlarged version of the character.

3 Click the Select button. Character Map places the selected character in the Characters To Copy text box.

4 Optionally, repeat steps 2 and 3 to add more characters to the Characters To Copy text box.

5 Click the Copy button. (This copies the selected characters to the **Clipboard.**)

6 Switch to the application that contains the document in which you want to place the special characters, position the **insertion point,** and then choose the application's Edit Paste command.

Fonts

Check Boxes Check boxes are on-off switches. They often look like little squares. If a check box is turned off, the little square is empty. If a check box is turned on, the little square shows a checkmark.

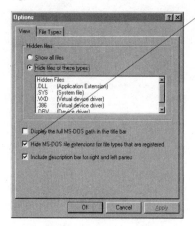

Windows 95 uses little checkmarks to mark check boxes, as do many Windows-based applications.

To turn on and off a check box, you can click the box.

You can also use the keyboard. For example, you can use the Tab key to select the check box and then press the Spacebar to turn on and off the check box. Or if the check box shows an underlined letter, you can also turn it on and off by pressing the Alt key and the underlined letter.

Click   The word "click" is a shortcut description for this two-step sequence:

1   You move the mouse pointer so that it rests over some object—such as a menu name.

2   You press and release the left mouse button. (It'll probably make a clicking sound as you do this.)

Rather than describe this two-step sequence half a billion times in a user guide, writers refer to the process as "clicking" the object. If you move the mouse pointer over a menu name and press and release the left mouse button, for example, you say that you "clicked" the menu name.

Double-Click; Drag; Right-Click

Clip Art Clip art refers to the pictures that you can paste into documents. Many word processors and drawing packages come with clip art images.

This clip art image comes with Microsoft Word. In keeping with the jungle-adventure motif of this book, I selected an elephant.

Clipboard Ever see the television show "Star Trek"? If you did, you may remember the transporter room. It let the Starship *Enterprise* move Captain Kirk, Mr. Spock, and nearly anyone or anything else just about anywhere. The Clipboard is the Windows 95 equivalent of the *Enterprise*'s transporter room. With the Clipboard, Windows 95 easily moves just about anything anywhere. When working with a Windows-based **application,** you can use the Clipboard to move chunks of text, tables, and even graphic images to and from different **files.** You can also use the Clipboard to move text, tables, and graphic images between Windows-based applications—such as from Microsoft Word to Microsoft Excel.

To move information around via the Clipboard, you use the Edit menu's Cut, Copy, Paste, and Paste Special commands—so you don't have to know all that much about the Clipboard to make good use of it. One thing you should remember about the Clipboard, however, is that it stores what you've copied or cut only temporarily. The next time you copy or cut, the previous Clipboard contents are replaced. And when you exit Windows 95 and turn off your computer, the Clipboard contents are erased.

🐾 **Clipboard Viewer; Copying Data; OLE**

Clipboard Viewer
Previous versions of Windows automatically installed an application called Clipboard Viewer. It let you see what was stored on the **Clipboard.** It also let you save the Clipboard's contents. Windows 95 doesn't install a Clipboard Viewer (unless you specifically tell it to). But you can still see what's on the Clipboard and store what's there using the **WordPad** application.

Viewing Clipboard Contents
To view the Clipboard contents, start WordPad and then choose the Edit Paste command. WordPad pastes the Clipboard contents into the WordPad **document**—where you can see them.

Saving Clipboard Contents
The contents of the Clipboard are stored only until the next time you copy or cut or until you exit Windows 95. If you don't want to lose the current Clipboard contents, paste the Clipboard contents into a WordPad document, as described earlier. Then to save the Clipboard contents, save the WordPad document.

Reusing Clipboard Contents
To reuse Clipboard contents you've previously stored in a WordPad document, open the WordPad document, select the stored Clipboard contents, and then choose the Edit Copy command to move the contents back to the Clipboard.

⁂ Clipboard; Copying Data; Opening Files; Saving Files

Clock
Earlier versions of Windows had a Clock application. It's probably still on your disk someplace. So you could start it if you wanted by using **Windows Explorer.** (The application's file name is CLOCK.EXE, by the way.)

But you shouldn't need the old Clock application. At the right end of the **Taskbar,** Windows 95 now displays the time for you.

This digital clock tells you the system time.

⁂ Dates and Times

Close Button

The Close button appears in the upper right corner of application windows and document windows as an "X" inside a box. It lets you close, or remove, a window from the screen. All you need to do is click the button.

This is the application window's Close button.

This is the document window's Close button.

Closing Documents; Window Buttons

Closing Applications ❖ Exiting Windows-Based Applications

Closing Documents

You close **documents** so that they don't consume **memory,** so that they don't clutter your screen, and so that they don't just plain annoy you.

Closing a Single Document

To close a single document, either click its **Close button** or be sure the document is visible and then choose its File Close command.

If There Are Unsaved Changes

Most **applications** won't close a document that you have changed but have not yet saved. The application first asks if you want to save your changes. If you say, "Well, yeah, that seems like a good idea," the application then saves the document.

C

Colors You can change the colors that Windows 95 uses for the parts of its windows, **dialog boxes,** and **message boxes.** **Right-click** the **desktop,** and then choose the Properties command from the **shortcut menu.** When Windows 95 displays the Display Properties dialog box, click the Appearance **tab.**

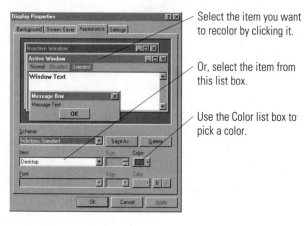

Select the item you want to recolor by clicking it.

Or, select the item from this list box.

Use the Color list box to pick a color.

Combo Box "Combo box" sounds like a special order from a fast food take-out place. But it's not. A combo box is part **text box** and part **list box.** You can, therefore, enter something in a combo box the way you enter something in a text box. Or you can activate a **drop-down list box** and select an entry from it.

Not that you care, but this is a combo box. You can enter something in this box, just as if it were a text box. Or you can activate the drop-down list and select one of its entries.

Command Buttons

Command Buttons Command buttons tell Windows-based **applications** that you either are or are not ready to do something. For example, every **dialog box** shows a command button that's labeled "OK." If you click the OK button, the Windows-based application knows that you're ready to move forward. So clicking OK is your way of giving the Windows-based application the thumbs-up signal.

Most dialog boxes also show the Cancel command button. Cancel means, basically, thumbs down.

Some dialog boxes also show the **Help** command button. Help means, well, that you need help, of course. When you click Help, the Windows-based application starts the Windows 95 Help application and attempts to turn to the right page of Help information.

Choosing Command Buttons

To choose a command button, you can use any of three methods. You can click the button using the mouse. You can use the Tab and Shift+Tab keys to highlight the command button with a dark border and then press Enter. (If the button already shows a dark border, you can simply press Enter.) Or if one of the letters in the command button name is underlined, you can press the Alt key and then the underlined letter.

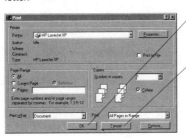

To choose the OK command button, simply press Enter.

To choose the Cancel command button, click it.

continues

Command Buttons *(continued)*

Displaying Additional Options

If the text on a command button is followed by greater than symbols (>>), clicking the button expands the currently displayed dialog box. If the text is followed by an ellipsis (...), clicking the button displays another dialog box. For example, the Properties command button in the last screen picture includes an ellipsis (Properties...).

Commands
You use commands to tell Windows-based **applications** what you want them to do. For example, you use a command to tell Windows 95 to exit, or close, an application. If an application prints **documents,** you use a command to tell the application you want it to print.

To make your life easier, Windows 95 organizes related commands into sets called **menus.**

Control Menu Commands; Menu Bars; Toolbars

Communications
Windows 95 comes with a bunch of cool tools for helping you communicate electronically. **HyperTerminal** lets you connect to another computer using a modem. Dial-Up Networking, or **Remote Access,** lets you connect your computer to a **network** using a modem. And Windows 95 also comes with built-in **mail.**

Compression
Windows 95 works with both the **DoubleSpace** and **DriveSpace** compression applications. A compression application, by the way, scrunches your data so that more of it fits on your **hard disk.** Windows 95 is a happier camper if you let it use DriveSpace. In fact, Windows 95 comes with a new version of DriveSpace.

Context Menus · Shortcut Menus

Control Menu Commands

Control menu commands appear, not surprisingly, on the Control menus of **application windows, document windows,** and some **dialog boxes.**

To open the Control menu of a window or a dialog box, you click the Control menu icon. (It's the little picture in the upper left corner of the window or the dialog box.)

This, by the way, is a Control menu.
You don't always see all these commands on a Control menu.
Windows 95 displays only those commands that make sense in the current situation.

Control menu commands let you manipulate the window or the dialog box in the following ways.

Restore

Undoes the last Minimize or Maximize command. Handy if you're fooling around with the Control menu and you make a terrible mistake.

Move

Tells Windows 95 you want to move the window or the dialog box. Windows 95, ever mindful of your feelings, changes the mouse pointer to a four-headed arrow. Once this happens, use the Up and Down arrow keys to change the screen position of the window or the dialog box. Press Enter when you've finished moving.

Size

Tells Windows 95 you want to change the size of the window. When you click this command, Windows 95 changes the mouse pointer to a four-headed arrow. You change the window size by using the Up and Down arrow keys to move the bottom border and by using the Left and Right arrow keys to move the right border. Press Enter when you've finished sizing.

continues

Control Menu Commands *(continued)*

Minimize

Tells Windows 95 in no uncertain terms that it should remove the window from the screen. Windows 95 follows your command, but to remind you of the minimized window, it leaves a button on the **Taskbar** or at the bottom of the application window. Simply **right-click** the Taskbar button to display its Control menu.

Maximize

Tells Windows 95 that it should make the window or the dialog box as big as it can. If you maximize an application window—such as Microsoft Word's—Windows 95 makes the application window as big as your screen. In many applications, by the way, document windows can be maximized so that they fill the application window.

Close

Removes the window or the dialog box from the screen. There's more to this command, however, than first meets the eye. If you close an application window, you actually close the application. If you close a document window, you also close the document displayed in the document window. If the document hasn't yet been saved, most applications ask if you want to do this before the document is closed. If you close a dialog box, it's the same as clicking the Cancel command button.

 **Closing Documents**

Control Panel Have you ever seen a news video that showed a nuclear reactor? You know how there's always that room with a bunch of people wearing white coats and hard hats? (Almost as if these will help in the case of a melt-down...) OK. Now, remember how there's always this big, huge control panel in the room with a bunch of lights and switches and gauges?

Windows 95 has a similar Control Panel that controls the way Windows 95 operates. Fortunately, you don't need to be a nuclear engineer to use Windows 95's Control Panel. To change one of these settings, you just open Control Panel (such as by clicking the **Start button** and next choosing Settings and then Control Panel). Then you click the appropriate Control Panel tool.

To change some aspect of how your computer works, you use one of these tools.

∴ Dates and Times; Regional Settings

C

Copying Data
You can copy data—such as a value—from one **application** to another or within a Windows-based application by placing it on the **Clipboard** and then pasting the data from the Clipboard to its new location. In general, you do this by selecting the data, choosing the Edit Copy command, positioning the **insertion point** where you want to place the data, and then choosing the Edit Paste command.

⁘ **Moving Data; Sharing Data Between Applications**

Copying Files
To copy **files,** you use **Windows Explorer.** To start Windows Explorer, click the **Start button.** Next choose Programs and then Windows Explorer.

Copying a File to a Floppy Disk Using the Mouse
To copy a file to a floppy disk using the mouse, follow these steps:

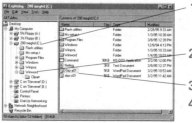

1 Click the disk drive icon of the drive that contains the file.

2 Click the folder that contains the file.

3 Click the file.

4 Drag the file to the floppy disk drive icon.

Copying a File to a Floppy Disk Using the File Send To Command
To copy a file to a floppy disk using File Send To, follow these steps:

1 Click the disk drive icon of the drive that contains the file.

2 Click the folder that contains the file.

3 Click the file.

4 Choose the File Send To command. Windows Explorer displays a menu that lists your computer's floppy disk drives.

5 Click the floppy disk drive.

Copying a File to Another Hard Disk Location Using the Mouse

To copy a file to another folder on your hard disk using the mouse, follow these steps:

1 Click the disk drive icon that contains the file.
2 Click the folder that contains the file.
3 Click the file.
4 Hold down the Ctrl key.
5 Drag the file to the folder you want to copy it to.

Copying a File Using the Edit Copy and Edit Paste Commands

To copy a file using Edit Copy and Edit Paste, follow these steps:

1 Click the disk drive icon that contains the file.
2 Click the folder that contains the file.
3 Click the file.
4 Choose the Edit Copy command.
5 Click the disk drive icon of the drive to which you want to copy the file.
6 Click the folder to which you want to copy the file.
7 Choose the Edit Paste command.

Copying multiple files

To copy multiple files, simply select multiple files. If you're copying files using the mouse, you can select multiple files by clicking the first file, holding down Shift, and then clicking the last file. Or you can also hold down Ctrl and then click each file.

 Moving Data

Curser   A curser is someone who curses, who frequently shares his (or her) vocabulary of obscenities. This isn't a book about manners or linguistics. So I'm not going to share my thoughts with you—nor what my parents told me the first time I brought home one of these special words from grade school. I do want you to know there's a difference between a curser and a **cursor**.

Cursor   People sometimes call the **insertion point** a "cursor." You can call it that if you want. One of the fun things about being an adult is that you usually get to make your own decisions. In this book, I'm going to call the insertion point an "insertion point."

Whatever you do, however, don't confuse the terms insertion point and **selection cursor**.

Dates and Times Your computer keeps its own calendar and clock. In fact, it's from this clock that Windows 95 gets the time it displays at the right end of the **Taskbar.** What's more, many Windows-based **applications** let you include the date and time from this calendar and clock in their **documents.** And Windows 95 tags files with the dates and times that you create and modify them.

Changing the Date or Time

You can change the time (and the date, too) by **right-clicking** the digital **clock.** When you do this, Windows 95 displays a menu. The first menu command is Adjust Date/Time. Choose this first command, and Windows 95 displays the Date/Time Properties dialog box.

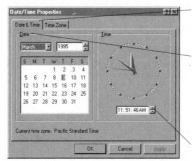

Click the Date & Time **tab** if you want to change the date or time.

To change the date, use the Date settings: the month drop-down list box, the year box, and the calendar that has the clickable days.

To change the time, use the Time box.

Changing the Time Zone

Click the Time Zone tab if you want to, you know, change the time zone.

To change the time zone, select a time zone from the drop-down list box.

You can also change the time zone by clicking the map. Try it.

continues

Dates and Times *(continued)*

The path not taken

There's another way to change the date and time, too. You can open the Control Panel folder and double-click the Date/Time tool.

Defragment Computers are funny about the way they store **files** on your disks. They tend to break up files and store the pieces all over the place. A chunk here. A chunk there. Another chunk someplace else, and so on. It can't be any huge surprise to you that retrieving files that have been fragmented this way is time-consuming and tedious. Windows 95 has to run all over the place, grabbing the little odds and ends of your files. Every so often, then, you'll want to check your disk's fragmentation.

Fortunately, there's a simple way to address this kooky situation. You can check a disk's fragmentation and defragment your disk using the Windows 95 Disk Defragmenter application. To do this, click the **Start button.** Then choose Programs, Accessories, System Tools, and Disk Defragmenter.

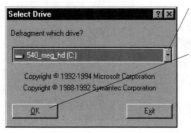

Identify the disk drive you want to defragment using this list box.

Click OK to begin the defragmentation. (If your disk isn't fragmented enough to warrant defragmentation, Disk Defragmenter tells you so and gives you the option of stopping the defragmentation.)

Background defragmentation

You can defragment a disk as a background activity. In other words, you can defragment a disk using the Disk Defragmenter application while you're doing work with another **application**. To switch to the other application, click its **task button**.

Deleting Files ❖ Erasing Files

Deleting Folders You can delete a **folder** and erase all of the files stored in that folder by using **Windows Explorer.** Start Windows Explorer, select the folder, and then choose File Delete.

Desktop The desktop is the background that appears beneath the application windows.

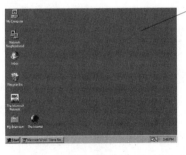

This background is the desktop.

Your desktop's appearance depends on the desktop pattern you selected and the **wallpaper** you've said Windows 95 should use to "paper over" the desktop pattern. (This is strange, right? Wallpaper on a desktop? I agree.)

You specify a desktop pattern or wallpaper using Control Panel's Display tool.

Device A device is something you plug into your computer. A good rule of thumb is that if this pluggable thing has a cable or screws, you've got a device. Otherwise, you don't. For example, tape drives, internal and external modems, floppy disk drives, and printers are all either screwed in or cabled. So they're devices.

Dialog Box A dialog box is simply an on-screen form you fill out to tell Windows 95 or some Windows-based application how it should complete some **command.** Any command name followed by an ellipsis (...) displays a dialog box.

 This is a dialog box.

Directory MS-DOS, the predecessor to Windows 95, used directories to organize your disks and the **files** they store. Windows 95 uses a similar tool, **folders.** For all practical purposes, you can think of Windows 95's new folders as equivalent to MS-DOS's old directories.

Disabilities Windows 95 has a whole bunch of **Control Panel** tools that you can install to make using computers easier for people who have disabilities. There are Control Panel tools that make it easier to use your mouse and keyboard, settings that convert audio warnings (like beeps) into visual cues, and settings that change the display so that it's easier to read.

To noodle around with any of this stuff, start Control Panel (such as by clicking the **Start button,** choosing Settings, and then choosing Control Panel). Then double-click the Accessibility Options tool.

Disk Caching Disk caching improves the speed with which your personal computer grabs (reads) data from and saves (writes) data to your **hard disk.** In Windows 95, disk caching is performed by **VCACHE.** We (you and I, that is) don't have time to get into some scholarly discussion of this disk-caching business. But you probably want to know a couple of things.

Caching Read Operations

Disk caching during read operations simply means that your personal computer grabs a bit more data than it really needs, with the idea that the next time your personal computer needs data it may already have it. Basically, caching read operations is akin to grabbing a handful of potato chips from the bowl even though at the moment you want to eat only one. When you want to eat that next chip, you won't have to reach for the bowl again.

Caching Write Operations

Disk caching during write operations simply means that your personal computer doesn't save data on your disk every time some eensy teensy bit changes. Instead, your computer accumulates these changes and then saves them in bigger chunks whenever it is idle. Basically, caching during write operations is like collecting garbage in a can under the sink and then emptying this garbage whenever the can gets full. (In no way, of course, do I mean to imply that your data is garbage. It's just the best simile I can think of.)

Documents A document is what gets displayed in the **document window** that an **application** displays. In the case of a word processor, this name works pretty nicely. The report, letter, or memo that a word processor displays in a document window is, well, basically a document. Right?

Unfortunately, the "document" label doesn't work as well when it's used to name the information that other applications display. The spreadsheet that a spreadsheet application such as Lotus 1-2-3 or Microsoft Excel displays is also, technically speaking, a document; it gets displayed in a document window. The checkbook register that an accounting application such as Quicken displays is, I guess, a document since it gets displayed in a document window.

Documents Submenu Windows 95 lists up to the last 15 documents you've used on its Documents submenu, which appears on the Start menu. You can open one of these documents (using the application that created the document, of course) by selecting the document from the submenu.

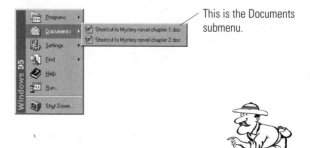

This is the Documents submenu.

Cleaning up the Documents submenu

You can remove all of the documents listed on the Documents submenu. Here's how. **Right-click** the **Taskbar,** and click the Properties command to display the Taskbar Properties dialog box. Click the Start Menu Programs tab. Then click the Clear command button.

Document Window The document window is the rectangle that an **application** uses to display your **documents.** If you have more than one document open, the **application window** stacks the documents, one on top of the other. You may not be able to see any but the active document window, however, unless you tile or cascade the open document windows or resize the top document window so that it doesn't fill the application window. (When you "tile" windows, you arrange them as squares on your screen—like the ceramic tiles around a bathtub or shower. When you "cascade" windows, you arrange them in a stack on your screen—but in a way that shows each document window's title bar.)

This is a document window.

Control Menu Commands

Double-Click To double-click an object simply means that you **click** it twice in a row. Quickly. Click-click.

Now that you know what double-click means, let me give you some examples of double-click operations. You can click a **minimized window** button to open its window. And you can double-click an unopened **document** or a document icon to start the associated **application** and open the document.

DoubleSpace MS-DOS versions 6.0 and 6.2 came with a disk compression application, DoubleSpace. It let you scrunch, or compress, a disk so that the **files** stored on that disk would take less disk space.

Windows 95 can work with disk drives you've compressed using DoubleSpace, but it would rather work with disk drives you've compressed using the newer **DriveSpace** application. DriveSpace, just for you history buffs, came with MS-DOS version 6.22 and replaced DoubleSpace. But Windows 95 supplies an updated version of DriveSpace called DriveSpace for Windows 95.

Drag

Drag is a shortcut description for this three-step sequence:

1 You move the mouse pointer so that it rests over some object—such as a **shortcut icon.**

2 You press and hold down the mouse's left button.

3 You move the mouse pointer. As you move the mouse pointer, Windows 95 moves, or drags, the object.

People in the know refer to the entire process as "dragging" the object. If you move a shortcut icon using the mouse, for example, you say that you "dragged" the icon.

Click; Double-Click; Drag-and-Drop

Drag-and-Drop

Drag-and-drop is a technique that lets you move and copy pieces of a document using the mouse. Drag-and-drop works in many spreadsheet and word processor applications.

Moving Using Drag-and-Drop

To move some piece of a document—such as a line of text, a paragraph, or a picture—select it, and then drag it to its new location.

Copying Using Drag-and-Drop

To copy some piece of a document—such as a chunk of text or a picture—select it, press Ctrl, and then drag it to its new location.

Sharing data between applications

You can often use drag-and-drop techniques to share data between **application windows.** Microsoft Word and Microsoft Excel, for example, let you drag-and-drop from their application windows. When you do, you create embedded objects.

Click; Drag; OLE

DriveSpace DriveSpace is the disk compression **application** that comes with Windows 95. With a little luck and a few minutes of your time, DriveSpace lets you almost double the size of your disk. (OK. It doesn't really double the size of your disk. It just stores everything more efficiently. You can store a bunch more stuff on a disk that's been compressed using DriveSpace.)

Compressing a Disk

To compress a disk using DriveSpace, follow these steps:

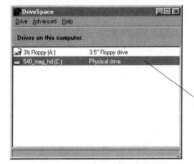

1 Start DriveSpace by clicking the **Start button.** Then choose Programs, Accessories, System Tools, and DriveSpace.

2 Use the Drives On This Computer list box to select the drive you want to compress.

3 Choose the Drive Compress command.

4 When Windows 95 displays the Compress A Drive dialog box, click Start.

continues

DriveSpace *(continued)*

Uncompressing a Disk

Uncompressing a disk works almost like compressing a disk. You start DriveSpace. You select the drive. And then you choose the Drive Uncompress command.

"But," I Ask, "Why Not?"

"Now, wait a minute," you're thinking. "Why would I want to uncompress a disk? This disk compression business seems like a good thing. Can someone ever really have too much disk space?"

Your question is a good one. But there is a reason why you might not want to compress a disk or might want to uncompress a previously compressed disk.

In a word, the reason is "performance." Disk compression utilities like DriveSpace can, in some cases, slow down your computer. This isn't always true. But your **microprocessor** goes to quite a bit of effort to scrunch data. If you've got a powerful microprocessor that isn't very busy doing other things, you may not even notice a performance degradation. But if you haven't got a powerful microprocessor or if your microprocessor is already working hard, it may not be able to effortlessly fit in extra work like disk compression and uncompression.

Drop-and-Drag This is the name of a TV show about hunting. It's on one of the cable stations. I mention this only so that you don't confuse the TV show with the similarly named feature available in many Windows-based applications, **drag-and-drop**.

By the way, "Drop-and-Drag," the television show, is often on after "Guten Tag." And, no, this isn't another show about hunting. It's a learn-the-German-language show.

E

Drop-Down List Boxes A drop-down list box is a **list box** that doesn't show its list until you tell it to. To tell a drop-down list box it should display its list, either click the down arrow at the end of the box or select the list box and then press Alt+Down arrow key.

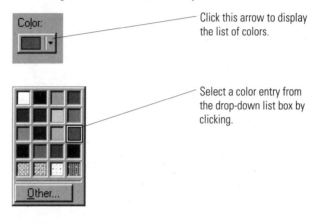

Click this arrow to display the list of colors.

Select a color entry from the drop-down list box by clicking.

Electronic Mail ❖ **Mail**

Erasing You can erase the preceding character, such as in a **text box** or **combo box,** by pressing the Backspace key. (The preceding character is the one in front of the **insertion point.**)

You can erase the current selection—a character, a word, or the contents of some text box—by pressing the Del key or the Backspace key. Some **applications** also provide an Edit Clear **command** for erasing a selection.

Erasing Files

Documents and other important **files** such as application files get stored as files on disk. To erase a file—such as a document file—in the Windows 95 operating system, you use **Windows Explorer.**

Erasing Files Using Windows Explorer

To erase a file once you've started Windows Explorer, follow these steps:

1 Click the disk drive icon of the drive that contains the file.

2 Click the folder, and, if necessary, double-click the folder within the folder that contains the file or files you want to erase.

3 Click the file or files you want to erase.

4 Choose the File Delete command.

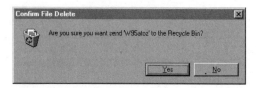

5 When Windows Explorer asks, confirm that you do want to delete the file. Windows Explorer then deletes it. If the file is on a **hard disk,** Windows 95 also places it in the **Recycle Bin.**

Exiting Windows 95

To exit Windows 95, click the **Start button,** and then choose Shut Down. Windows 95 displays the Shut Down Windows dialog box. You click the appropriate **option button** and then click Yes.

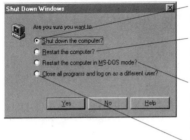

To exit Windows 95, click this button.

To exit Windows 95 and then restart it, click this button.

To shut down Windows 95 and then restart your computer using MS-DOS, click this button.

To end the current session, stop any running applications, and then log on as another user, click this button.

❖ **Exiting Windows-Based Applications**

Exiting Windows-Based Applications

To exit just about any Windows-based application, you can choose the File Exit command. Or you can close the **application window** by clicking its **Close button.** In general, an application asks if you want to save **documents** that have unsaved changes.

❖ **Closing Documents; Saving Files**

Explorer ❖ **Windows Explorer**

File   **Applications** and **documents** get stored on disk as files. For example, the document file you create with **WordPad** gets stored on disk as a file. And the **Windows Explorer** application gets stored on disk as a file.

File Manager   Earlier versions of Windows used the File Manager application to copy, move, and delete files. It also let you format and label **floppy disks**.

Windows 95 replaces File Manager with **Windows Explorer.** Windows Explorer is more powerful and much handier to use. So I'm not going to describe here how File Manager works.

In love with File Manager?

If you really like File Manager and want to keep on using it, you should know that File Manager still exists in your Windows 95 **folder,** which is probably called Windows. Its file name is WINFILE.EXE. You can add WINFILE.EXE to the **Start menu.** Or you can create a **shortcut icon** for it.

File Names   You usually give a **document** its file name when you use the application's File Save As command.

File-Naming Rules

Windows 95 lets you name a **file** just about anything you want. You can use up to 255 characters, and you can use any characters you want except these:

\ / : , ; * ? " < > |

Spaces are acceptable.

Long File Names vs. Short File Names

OK. These new long file names that Windows 95 provides are great. But you still may want to access a file using MS-DOS (using another computer, for example), and you still may want to use earlier versions of Windows-based **applications** that think file names have to be 8 characters long. Because of this, Windows 95 actually uses two names for your files—a long file name that Windows 95 uses and a short file name that MS-DOS applications and earlier versions of Windows-based applications use.

Short file names, predictably, need to follow the old MS-DOS file-naming rules. A short file name can't have more than 8 characters. All numbers and letters that appear on your keyboard are OK. And so are many other characters. You can't, however, use characters that MS-DOS expects to be used in special ways on its command line such as spaces and all those other crazy characters that Windows 95 doesn't accept.

For files that use a long file name, Windows 95 automatically creates the short file name for you using the first 6 characters of the long file name, a tilde (~), and a number. If you name a file something like "Budget for 1994," for example, Windows 95 creates the short file name, "Budget~1."

Specifying File Extensions

The file extension isn't something you need to worry about. Windows-based applications supply the file extension to identify the file type. Microsoft Word, for example, uses the file extension DOC. Microsoft Excel uses the file extension XLS.

Because you don't need to worry about the file extension, Windows 95 often doesn't list it or show it. If you use **Windows Explorer** to look at the files in a **folder,** for example, you usually don't see any file extensions. The file extension does still exist, however. (Windows 95 uses the file extension to identify which application opens the file.)

File Pane If you start **Windows Explorer,** Windows 95 displays a window that shows the stuff that's connected to your computer—including any **folders** and **files.** This window is split into two chunks called "panes."

I need a way to refer to these panes. Since the right pane is the only one that shows files, I decided to call it the "file pane." I should admit that this is just something I've made up. I don't think you'll see this term anyplace else.

 Folder Pane

Floppy Disks Floppy disks don't really flop. So I don't know why they're called floppy disks. "Plastic disks" would probably be a better name. Because that's what they are. Floppy disks are those plastic, square disks you buy in boxes of 10 or 20 or whatever.

But the name isn't the only kooky part of these disks. There's also the size. The floppy disks that are the biggest in physical size (5.25 inches square) actually hold fewer bytes—either 360 KB or 1.2 MB. (KB stands for **kilobyte,** and MB stands for **megabyte.**) The smaller floppy disks (3.5 inches square) hold either 720 KB or 1.44 MB. Go figure.

Folder Windows 95 uses folders to organize your disks and the files they store. (Folders, by the way, replace **directories.**) You can also organize the files in a folder by creating folders within a folder. Basically, these folders work like the drawers in a filing cabinet.

You can create folders and see which folders organize the files on a disk by using **Windows Explorer.**

+• **Subfolder**

Folder Pane I use the term "folder pane" to refer to the left half of the **window** that **Windows Explorer** displays to show you what's connected to your computer, how the active disk's folders are organized, and which files are in the active folder.

+• **File Pane**

Fonts

Windows 95 lets you use a variety of fonts in your documents. With fonts, you can even add Greek symbols and other special characters to your document. (You do all this font fancywork within a Windows-based application—usually by using a command named something like Format Font.)

You can preview a font by starting **Windows Explorer,** opening the Fonts folder by clicking it, and then opening one of the fonts by double-clicking its icon.

❖ **PostScript**

Foreground Application

Windows 95 lets you run more than one **application** at a time. The foreground application is the application that your commands affect and that has the most visible or only visible window—it appears in front of the other **application windows** on your screen.

You can change which application runs in the foreground by clicking the **task button** of a **background application.**

People sometimes refer to a foreground application as the "active application" because it appears in what Windows 95 terms an "active window." This isn't a very good description, however. Any background applications that you or Windows 95 started are also active.

❖ **Multitasking; Switching Tasks**

Formatting Floppy Disks
You use **Windows Explorer** to format **floppy disks.**

Formatting a Floppy Disk

To format a floppy disk after you've started Windows Explorer and inserted the floppy disk in its drive, follow these steps:

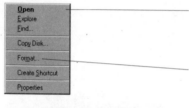

1 Right-click the floppy disk drive icon. Windows 95 displays a menu.

2 Choose Format. Windows 95 displays a dialog box.

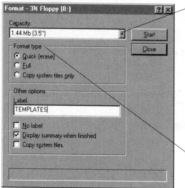

3 Use the Capacity drop-down list box to select the correct floppy disk drive capacity. (If this sounds like Greek or, worse, like Geek, just read the floppy disk label. It'll probably give the floppy disk drive capacity.)

4 Optionally, use the Format Type option buttons to specify which type of format you want. If you don't know what you want here, let Windows 95 pick for you.

5 Click Start. Windows Explorer displays a progress bar at the bottom of the screen to show you the formatting operation's progress.

6 Click Close when Windows Explorer finishes—unless, of course, you want to format another disk.

Games   Windows 95 comes with several games—Free Cell, Hearts,
Minesweeper, Party Line, and Solitaire—that you get to
by clicking the Start button and then choosing Programs,
Accessories, and Games. You don't get all of Windows 95's
games unless you install Windows 95 from a CD.

Click the deck to see your
next card.

Drag cards to move them
to another stack.

I'm not going to describe here how you play these games.
Mostly, you just click and drag. I will say, however, that
the games provide a pretty good way to get comfortable
with your mouse.

This last little nugget of knowledge also suggests a useful
explanation in case your boss wonders why you're fooling
around. "Oh, geez, Boss, I didn't know you were standing
behind me... Well, no, I'm not playing games. No way. I
just read in that Field Guide that you can hone your
mouse skills this way."

Gigabyte   A gigabyte is roughly 1000 **megabytes.** Since a
megabyte is roughly 1000 **kilobytes,** it also follows that
a gigabyte is roughly 1 million kilobytes. That's big.
Really big. But it's more than just big. It's also relevant.
Windows 95 lets you use up to 4 GB of **memory.** (People
use the abbreviation "GB" to stand for gigabyte.) And
Windows 95 also lets you use **hard disks** up to 137 GB
in size.

Groups

The previous version of Windows used **Program Manager** to organize your **applications** into sets—in a manner akin to the way your parents may have organized your clothes in a dresser when you were younger. Socks. Underwear. Shirts. You get the picture, right? These sets were called "groups."

I'm not sure why I've even told you this, however. Groups don't appear in Windows 95. Any groups you used to have will now show up as items on the Programs submenu of the **Start menu**.

In love with Program Manager?

If you really like Program Manager and want to keep on using it, you should know that Program Manager still exists in your Windows **folder**. Its file name is PROGMAN.EXE. You can add PROGMAN.EXE to the **Start menu**. Or you can create a **shortcut icon** for it.

Hard Disk

Inside your computer is a disk drive called a "hard disk." I have no idea why they're called hard disks. A better name would probably be "big disk." Hard disks hold much, much more data than **floppy disks.** You can get hard disks, for example, that store as much stuff as do ten thousand floppy disks.

⁘ **Gigabyte; Kilobyte; Megabyte**

Help

Windows 95 itself and almost all Windows-based applications include an online Help feature that almost always gives you information with just a click or a keystroke. You access this help by using one of the Help menu commands. The Help menu usually appears as the rightmost menu on an application's **menu bar.**

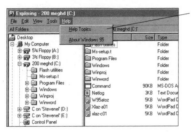

Help menus vary, but most of them closely resemble the Windows Explorer Help menu shown here.

Using the Help Topics Command

Choose the Help Topics command to display a list of the major categories of Help topics. When you do, Windows 95 starts the Help application and displays the Help Index. You can also click the Contents tab to display the Help table of contents.

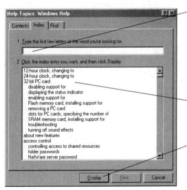

To find a Help topic in the Index, type the first few characters of the topic name. If you wanted help on Help, for example, you could type *help*.

To see information on one of the topics that Help lists, click that topic.

Click Display to see the first screen of Help information.

continues

Help *(continued)*

When you see one of these clickable buttons on a Help screen—they're called "**shortcut buttons**"—it means you can click here to get more information or to move to whatever dialog box is being discussed.

Getting back to the Contents list

Click the Contents tab to return to the index of Help topics—the same list you see when you click the Help Topics command.

Using the Help Find Command

Click the Find tab if you want to search through all the Help file information for any topics that use a specific word or phrase. (When you first click Find, you see a different dialog box than the one shown below. You need to press Enter once or twice to see this dialog box.)

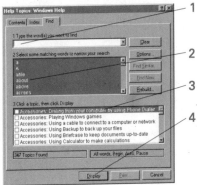

1 Type the word you want to find all uses of here.

2 You can also select a word from this list box.

3 Select the topic from the bottom list box.

4 Click Display.

About the Help About Command

The Help About command doesn't really give help.

The Help About command displays information about the application and, in some cases, about the system resources.

 Help Glossary

Help Glossary

If you see a colored term with a dotted under-line in the Help **application window,** it means there's a glossary entry, or definition, for the term.

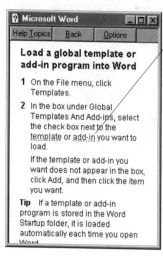

To see the definition, click the term.

Help displays glossary information in a **pop-up box.** Press any key or click anywhere to close the pop-up box.

HyperTerminal

HyperTerminal is Windows 95's powerful new communications **application.** With it and a modem, you can connect your computer to another computer, to an electronic mail service, and to many electronic bulletin board systems.

Describing a HyperTerminal Connection

To start HyperTerminal and use it to connect to another computer, you first need to describe the connection. To do this, follow these steps:

1 Click the **Start button.** Next choose Programs, Accessories, and then HyperTerminal Connections.

2 Start HyperTerminal by double-clicking the HyperTrm icon. HyperTerminal starts and asks you for the name of the connection.

3 Name the HyperTerminal connection using the Name text box.

4 If you want, you can also pick an icon using the Icon box.

5 Click OK. HyperTerminal asks you for the telephone number—and for some other information as well.

continues

HyperTerminal *(continued)*

6   Type the telephone number in the Phone Number box. (If neces-
    sary, you can also specify the country code and area code using the
    other boxes.)

7   Verify that the Connect Using drop-down list box specifies your
    modem.

8   Click OK. HyperTerminal asks for just a bit more information so that
    it can dial the telephone number.

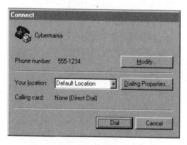

9   Click Dialing Properties if this is a long-distance telephone call and
    you'll need to fiddle with things like calling cards or if you'll need
    to precede the telephone number with a number in order to get an
    outside line. Use the dialog box that HyperTerminal displays to
    specify these extra bits of telephone trivia.

10 To dial the telephone number so that you can connect to the other
    computer, click Dial.

Saving the HyperTerminal Connection Description

You'll want to save the HyperTerminal connection description. To do so, follow these steps:

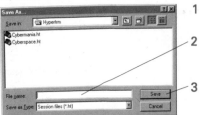

1 Choose the File Save As command.

2 Type a file name for the HyperTerminal description.

3 Click Save.

Connecting to Another Computer

Once you've described a connection, connecting subsequent times is easy. First, you click the **Start button.** Then choose Programs, Accessories, and HyperTerminal Connections.

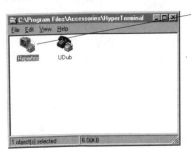

To connect, double-click a connection description. HyperTerminal displays the Dial dialog box (which I just showed). You click Dial to start HyperTerminal and connect to the other computer.

Once you start HyperTerminal, you see the HyperTerminal **application window** on your screen. To connect to the other computer, you need to do whatever it wants—probably provide a user name and password, for example.

continues

HyperTerminal *(continued)*

Working Once You're Connected

Once you connect to another computer, your computer is, essentially, just a "dumb terminal." In other words, you use your keyboard and your monitor, but it's really the other computer and its software that you're using. If you connect to a bulletin board system, for example, you'll probably see menus of commands that you can use to do different stuff.

Downloading Files

To move files from the computer to which you're connected to your computer, you first tell the other computer that you want it to send a file or a batch of files.

If you're using the Zmodem **protocol,** that's all you have to do. HyperTerminal displays a dialog box that reports on the file being sent from the other computer.

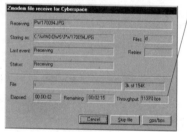

You can tell how fast the transfer is going by looking at the Throughput box.

If you're using some other protocol, you tell the other computer that you want it to send a file. Then—usually after you've been prompted by the other computer—you choose the Transfer Receive File command.

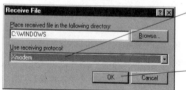

Activate this drop-down list box to specify the protocol as Xmodem, Kermit, or whatever.

Click OK after you pick a protocol.

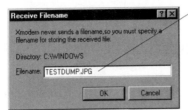

Name the file you will receive.

Zmodem is best

If you have a choice of file transfer protocols, choose Zmodem. Zmodem is easier to use because you don't have to mess with the protocol or name the files you're receiving. Zmodem lets you receive more than one file at a time. And best of all, Zmodem is much, much faster than other protocols. For example, one afternoon when I should have been working but was instead surfing the **Internet,** my throughput using Zmodem was around 16,000 bps, but my throughput using Xmodem was around 4,000 bps (bits per second).

Uploading Files

To send a file from your computer to the other computer, first do whatever gets the other computer ready. Then choose the Transfer Send File command. HyperTerminal displays a dialog box that asks for the file name and location and which file transfer protocol you want to use.

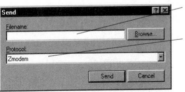

Identify the file and its location.

Choose a file transfer protocol.

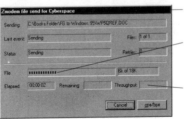

This dialog box describes the file transfer progress.

This progress bar shows you how far along the file transfer is.

The Throughput box shows you how fast files are transferring.

continues

77

HyperTerminal *(continued)*

Describing the Communications Protocol

With Windows 95, you usually don't have to worry about the communications protocol. Windows 95 examines your modem, figures out what it can do, and then works with the other computer to make your communications as fast and smooth as possible.

This means you shouldn't ever have to worry about things like data bits, stop bits, parity, and flow control. Sure. These details are important to Windows 95. They describe how the data is transmitted between your computer and the one it's connected to. But Windows 95 usually takes care of them.

Disconnecting from Another Computer

To disconnect from another computer, first complete any disconnection instructions provided by the electronic mail service or bulletin board system. Then choose the Call Disconnect command.

Icons

An icon is simply a visual image, or picture, that represents something else. In Windows 95 and Windows-based **applications,** icons represent such things as shortcuts and **documents.**

Recycle Bin

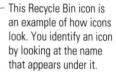

This Recycle Bin icon is an example of how icons look. You identify an icon by looking at the name that appears under it.

Microsoft
WinNews

This is a **shortcut icon.** It represents a document, or file. Clicking this shortcut icon tells Windows 95 to start the application that created the document and then tells that application to open the document.

This is a snake.

Inbox   Inbox is Windows 95's souped up electronic mail and fax messaging system. With Inbox, you can send and receive e-mail (as it's called) over virtually any e-mail system.

In-Place Editing   If you embed an **object** created by another **application** into a **document**—let's call this other application the "source application"—and if the source application supports in-place editing, you can edit the object by double-clicking it. When you **double-click** the object, the active application's menu bar and **toolbar** are merged with the source application's menu bar and toolbar. You can then use these menu commands and tools to edit the object. To return to the active application, click any part of the document except the object.

In-place editing is particularly handy when you're working with an application—like Microsoft PowerPoint—that uses lots of objects created with other applications. Why? Because you can make changes to all the objects without having to start a bunch of other applications.

 OLE

Insertion Point   The insertion point is the small vertical bar that shows where what you type gets placed. If this seems unclear to you, start a Windows-based **application** such as **WordPad,** begin typing, and look at the bar that moves ahead of the text you type. See it? That's the insertion point.

 Selection Cursor

International Settings **Regional Settings**

Internet The Internet is a **network** of networks that stretches around the world. As long as you're working on a computer that's connected to one of these networks, you can do all sorts of cool stuff. I'm now going to do something that I never do. Er, almost never do. I'm going to plug another book I've written, *Field Guide to the Internet.* Now, I'm not trying to trick you out of your hard-earned money. But if you're really interested in the Internet, you may want to know that *Field Guide to the Internet* describes in detail how Windows 95 users can surf the Internet. You can order *Field Guide to the Internet* by calling 1-800-MS-PRESS. Or you can buy it at any good bookstore.

Keyboard Shortcuts Keyboard shortcuts are key combinations you can use to select menu commands. So rather than having to open a **menu,** choose a **command** from the menu, and then press Enter, you simply press two or three keys. Often, the Alt or Ctrl key is one of those used.

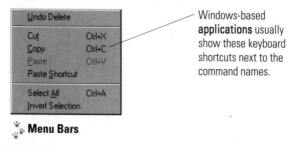

Windows-based **applications** usually show these keyboard shortcuts next to the command names.

Menu Bars

Kilobyte I know you didn't buy this book to learn about the guts of your computer. But since I've used the term "kilobyte" in a couple of places, I thought I should at least describe it. OK? Good. A byte is an 8-digit string of 1s and 0s that your computer uses to represent a character. This string of digits, for example, is a byte:

01010100

A kilobyte is roughly 1000 of these bytes. (Or to be excruciatingly precise, a kilobyte is exactly 1024 of these bytes.)

Gigabyte; Megabyte

Laptop Computers No, I'm not going to tell you what a laptop computer is. I know you know it's one of those portable computers that people lug around airports, all the time worrying that someone will steal it.

I do want you to know that Windows 95 provides several cool features just for laptop users: **Battery Meter, Brief-case, local connections,** and a hot docking ability so that you can disconnect (and reconfigure) your laptop from a docking station without turning it off. (You do need to choose the Eject PC command from the **Start menu.**)

.: **Remote Access**

List Boxes If there are only a limited set of choices that make sense in a given situation and a Windows-based application knows those choices, it displays a list. Your life is then easier—all you have to do is select one or more of the list's entries.

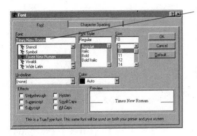

This list box shows **font** choices. You choose a font by clicking the font name in the list box using the mouse or by using the keyboard.

Selecting a Single List Entry

You can select a single list entry by clicking it. Or you can select a single list entry by highlighting it using the arrow keys.

Selecting Multiple List Entries

You can select a contiguous range of list entries in some list boxes by clicking the first list entry and then dragging the mouse to the last list entry. You can also highlight the first list entry, hold down the Shift key, and then press the Down arrow key to select additional list entries.

If you want to select a noncontiguous set of list entries, hold down the Ctrl key and then click the entries you want to select.

continues

L

List Boxes *(continued)*

Activating a Drop-Down List Box

If a Windows-based application doesn't have room to display a list box—and this is the usual case—it uses a **drop-down list box**. In this case, you don't see the list until you activate, or drop down, the list by clicking its arrow.

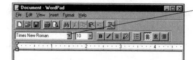 This is a drop-down list box.

Reviewing your choices

You can usually move to a list entry by typing its first character. For example, if you're at the start of a list and are viewing the entries that begin with the letter "A," but you want to move to the last part of the list and view the entries that be-gin with the letter "Z," type *Z*.

∴ Combo Boxes

Local Connections
You can connect two computers—such as your desktop computer and your **laptop computer**— with a parallel or serial cable. To make such a connection (after you've plugged in the cable), click the **Start button** and choose Programs, Accessories, and Direct Cable Connection. Then follow the on-screen instructions.

Local Reboot
If one of your **applications** hangs, or goes bonkers, you can perform what's called a "local reboot." This terminates the hung application without goofing up any of the other applications you've got running.

To perform a local reboot, press Ctrl+Alt+Del. In other words, press those three keys—Ctrl, Alt, and Del—at the same time. When Windows 95 displays the Close Appli-cation dialog box, follow these steps:

1 Click the application you want to close. (Windows 95 identifies any applications that aren't responding as "not responding.")
2 Click End Task

Logon You log on a computer running Windows 95. I know. This is new compared with earlier versions of Windows and with **MS-DOS.** Mostly, Windows 95 does this in case you're also logging on to a **network.** But it's also a sort of configuration thing for computers that are shared by more than one person. (Windows 95 lets you create different user profiles for different user names.)

This logon business shouldn't be construed as a security measure. Anyone can log on to your computer simply by providing a new user name and password.

Mail Windows 95 supports electronic mail in a big way. From within Windows 95, you can easily send electronic messages to other users on your **network.** If you're connected to the **Internet,** you can also send messages to other Internet users. Finally, if you use an online service like CompuServe or The Microsoft Network, hey, guess what? You can send messages using it, too.

There's more to this electronic mail business than I can cover in a few sentences, however. So if you're connected to a network, ask the network administrator for help. Or if you're using an online service, see the service's user documentation.

Media Player You use the Media Player **application** to play **multimedia** files—such as those that use sound or **animation**—and to control multimedia devices—such as compact disc or videodisc players. To use Media Player, click the **Start button.** Then choose Programs, Accessories, Multimedia, and Media Player.

Megabyte As you may already know, a byte is an 8-digit string of 1s and 0s that your computer uses to represent a character.

A **kilobyte** is roughly 1000 of these bytes. (Or to be precise, a kilobyte is exactly 1024 of these bytes.)

A megabyte is roughly 1 million of these bytes. (Or, again, to be absolutely precise, a megabyte is 1,048,576 bytes. Oh my.)

Memory Memory is the temporary storage area your computer uses while it runs Windows 95 and **applications.** What is stored in memory is lost when you turn off your computer. So that's kind of a bummer. But you can usually store stuff permanently by saving it on a disk.

∴ **Saving Files; Virtual Memory**

Menu Bars The menu bar is the row of **menu** names that usually appears beneath the application **title bar.** You will notice a similarity when you compare menu bars in Windows-based applications from the same software developer. Microsoft's Windows-based applications, for example, tend to use the same sorts of menus, as do Lotus Development's Windows-based applications.

 The menu bars in Microsoft's Windows-based applications often look the same. This is the Word menu bar.

∴ **Commands; Toolbars**

Menus Menus list **commands.** Ideally, menus are supposed to organize commands into sets of related commands.

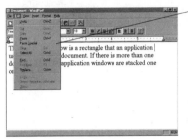

This is the WordPad Edit menu. Activate it by clicking it or by pressing Alt and the underlined letter in the menu name, E.

⁖ Menu Bars; Submenus; Toolbars

Message Box A message box is simply a miniature **dialog box** that displays a message from a Windows-based application. It also usually displays some **command buttons,** such as OK and Cancel.

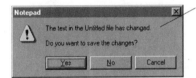

This is the message box that **Notepad** displays if you try to close a **document** that has unsaved changes. Rather than OK and Cancel, it uses Yes, No, and Cancel command buttons.

Microprocessor A microprocessor is the engine that powers your computer. It's the microprocessor, for example, that does things like add numbers and manipulate chunks of data.

Most IBM compatible personal computers, by the way, use microprocessors made by Intel, such as the 80386, 80486, and Pentium.

Microsoft Network
The Microsoft Network is Microsoft's global online service. With Windows 95 and a **modem**, you can connect to The Microsoft Network.

Minimized Windows
A minimized window is one that you've told Windows 95 to shrink so that it shows as a button.

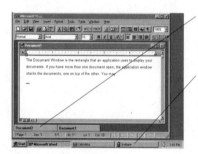

Minimized **document windows** appear as buttons at the bottom of the **application window**.

Minimized application windows (and all other running applications, too) appear as buttons on the **Taskbar**.

Minimizing Windows
To minimize a document window or an application window, either choose the Minimize command from the window's Control menu or click the Minimize button in the upper right corner of the window.

Unminimizing Windows
To restore a shrunken document window, click the document window's Maximize button.

To restore a shrunken application window, click the application window's Maximize button on the Taskbar.

Control Menu Commands; Window Buttons

Modem A modem is just a **device** that connects your computer to a telephone line. You need a modem for connecting to online services and for connecting to another computer or network using **remote access.**

Moving Data You can move data—such as a chunk of text—from one application to another or within a Windows-based application. You do this by cutting the data to place it on the **Clipboard** and then pasting the data from the Clipboard to its new location. In general, to do this cutting and pasting, you select the data, choose the Edit Cut command (or press Shift+Del or Ctrl+X), position the **insertion point** at the place you want to move the data, and then choose the Edit Paste command (or press Shift+Ins or Ctrl+V).

> ⁘ **Copying Data; Sharing Data Between Applications**

Moving Files You use **Windows Explorer** to move **files.** To start Windows Explorer, click the **Start button.** Next choose Programs and then Windows Explorer.

Moving a File to Another Hard Disk Location Using the Mouse

To move a file to another location on your **hard disk** using the mouse, follow these steps:

1 Click the disk drive icon of the disk that contains the file you want to move.

2 Click the **folder,** and, if necessary, double-click the **subfolder** that contains the file.

3 Click the file.

4 Drag the file to the folder or subfolder where you want to move it.

continues

Moving Files *(continued)*

Moving a File Using Commands

To move a file by using commands, follow these steps:

1 Click the disk drive icon of the disk that contains the file you want to move.

2 Click the folder that contains the file.

3 Click the file.

4 Choose the Edit Cut command.

5 Click the disk drive icon of the disk to which you want to move the file.

6 Click the folder to which you want to move the file.

7 Choose the Edit Paste command.

Copying Files

MS-DOS In the old days—before Windows 95—you started MS-DOS first. Then, after it was running, you used MS-DOS to start Windows. Everything is different nowadays, however. Windows 95 runs all by itself. You turn on your computer, and away it goes.

Curiously, however, Windows 95 comes with a new version of MS-DOS. Even more curiously, if you've got MS-DOS **applications** that you want to run, Windows 95 will probably run them better than MS-DOS did because it sets up things called **virtual machines.**

Booting Using MS-DOS

MS-DOS Prompt The MS-DOS Prompt command, which appears on the Programs menu, displays the MS-DOS command prompt. You use it to do whatever you do with the MS-DOS command prompt—such as type MS-DOS commands.

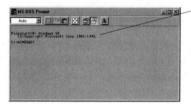

Here's what you see if you choose the MS-DOS Prompt command on the Programs menu: the MS-DOS command prompt displayed in its own window.

When you're done type *exit* at the prompt.

MSN ∴ Microsoft Network

Multimedia "Multimedia" is one of those in-vogue buzzwords that people throw around a lot these days. Technically, it refers to a product that uses multiple mediums for communication. A new Tony Bennett CD, for example, uses one communication medium: music. And a book on music uses another communication medium: text in the form of ink on paper. If you combine the music with the text, you have multiple mediums—a.k.a., multimedia.

Practically speaking, what people mean when they refer to multimedia is compact discs, or CDs, that use multiple mediums for communication: text, music and other sound, animation, video, and anything else the multimedia author can talk the multimedia publisher into.

All of this relates to Windows 95 in a pretty big way because multimedia **applications** are real resource hogs. Windows 95 makes running these hogs much more manageable, however, because it's a real work horse.

To play a multimedia CD, you need to have a multimedia-capable computer, which usually uses a CD player, a sound card, and some speakers.

Multitasking Multitasking refers to running more than one
application at a time. You may not care about this, but
Windows 95 lets you multitask. Windows 95
automatically multitasks Windows-based applications.
Whenever Windows 95 or you open, or start, more than
one Windows-based application, you're multitasking.
(Pretty cool, huh?)

To switch between the applications you're running, you
click application **task buttons** on the **Taskbar.** You can
also press Alt+Tab to cycle, or jump, through the applications you've started.

 **Switching Tasks**

My Computer My Computer is simply a picture of your computer. You double-click the My Computer icon on the
desktop to see other **icons** that represent the various parts
of your computer. You can then double-click any of those
icons to get information about or use that particular part.

This is a picture of my
computer.

Properties; Shell

Network A network is a bunch of computers that are connected. Windows 95 lets you create what are called "peer-to-peer networks"—as long as you've got network cards installed in the computers and the right kind of cabling to connect the network cards.

The cool thing about networks is that they make it easy to share equipment like **printers** and information like **files.** If your computer is part of a network, you can see icons for all the computers on the network by double-clicking the **Network Neighborhood** icon.

Network Neighborhood The Network Neighborhood gives the big picture of the network your computer is connected to. To see this picture, double-click the Network Neighborhood icon, which appears on the desktop if you're connected to a network.

Notepad Windows 95 provides a simple text editor called Notepad. Notepad isn't anything fancy. But it is handy. You can use it, for example, to jot down quick notes.

Starting Notepad

To start Notepad, click the **Start button**. Then choose Programs, Accessories, and Notepad.

continues

Notepad *(continued)*

Creating a Note

To create a note, simply begin typing using the keyboard.

If you want Notepad to **word wrap** your lines of text, choose the Edit Word Wrap command.

To edit text you've already entered, first select the character or block of text you want to change. (You can do this by clicking just before the first character you want to change and then dragging the mouse to just after the last character you want to change.) Next type the new text that will replace the old text.

You can erase the preceding character by pressing Backspace.

To erase the current selection—a character, a sentence, or a paragraph—press Del.

Finding Text

Choose the Search Find command to find text within a **document.**

Choose the Search Find Next command to repeat the last search you specified using the Search Find command.

Printing a Note

Choose the File Print command to print the note.

Opening Files; Saving Files; WordPad

Date-stamping and time-stamping notes

If you use LOG (instead of TXT) as the file extension for a note and type *.LOG* at the left margin of the note's top line, Notepad automatically adds lines of text to the end of the note that give the date and time the Notepad file was last modified. You can also place the current system date and time in a note by using the Edit Time/Date command.

Object   The word "object" gets my vote as the most overused and therefore least useful technoterm. It is used in at least a dozen different ways. In drawing applications, the term "object" often refers to the lines and shapes you draw. In some database applications, "object" refers to the building blocks that comprise your database. In programming, the term can refer to items that your application manipulates. In Windows 95, "object" sometimes refers to the things you see on the **desktop.** And, oh yes. The term "object" is also used to refer to OLE objects, which are chunks of **documents** that you copy or move between **applications.**

⁙ OLE

OLE   OLE lets you share stuff between **documents.** Oh, sure. "Stuff" doesn't sound like a very precise term. But it's tough to be precise about what you can do with OLE because you can share just about anything. Let me explain.

You use OLE to create what's called a "compound document"—a document file that combines two or more types of information. For example, you might want to create a compound document that includes a long report written in Microsoft Word. On page 27 of your report, however, you might want to include a worksheet (or a worksheet fragment) created in Lotus 1-2-3. And perhaps on page 37 of your report, you might want to include a chart created in Microsoft Excel.

You could add other sorts of objects—such as recorded sounds. So your compound document would really consist of stuff created in different **applications** and pasted together into one big compound document.

continues

OLE *(continued)*

Using OLE to Create Compound Documents

To do all this pasting and combining, you can often use the application's Edit Copy and Edit Paste (or Edit Paste Special) commands. Microsoft applications such as Excel and Word also include Insert Object commands that let you add and create objects for a compound document. You indicate whether you want an object linked or embedded when you use the Edit Paste, Edit Paste Special, or Insert Object command.

Distinguishing Between Linked Objects and Embedded Objects

A linked object—remember, this might be the Excel chart you've pasted into a word processor document—gets updated whenever the source document changes. An embedded object doesn't. (You can, however, double-click an embedded object to open the application that created the embedded object and make your changes.)

What you absolutely need to know about OLE

Perhaps the most important tidbit for you to know about OLE is that it's easy to use. You don't have to do anything other than copy and paste the things—called objects—that you want to plop into the compound document. If you're working with applications that support the newest version of OLE, you may also be able to **drag-and-drop** objects between application windows.

Opening Files
You can open both application files and document files. You do this using either the **Start button** or **Windows Explorer.**

Opening Application Files

You open application files when you start the application—for example, by choosing the application from the Programs menu or from one of its **submenus.** You can also open an application by double-clicking an application file listed in Windows Explorer's **file pane.**

Opening Document Files

You open document files so that you can modify the stuff, or data, that's in the files. You usually open document files by starting the application that created the document and then using that application's File Open command.

To use an application's File Open command, you usually follow steps like those described below for opening a **WordPad** file:

1 In WordPad, choose the File Open command.

2 Type the file name for the document file.

3 If necessary, use the Look In drop-down list box to specify where the file is located.

4 If necessary, use the Files Of Type drop-down list box to specify what kind of file you're looking for.

5 Click Open.

Opening Document Files Using Windows Explorer

If you double-click a document file listed in the Windows Explorer window and Windows Explorer knows which application created the document, Windows Explorer opens the application and then tells it to open the document file.

To tell Windows Explorer which application created a document file, you choose the View Options command and then click the File Types tab to display the Options dialog box. Next, you click the New Type command button and use the Add New File Type dialog box, which Windows 95 displays, to describe which application opens a particular type of file.

continues

Opening Files *(continued)*

Opening Document Files Using a Shortcut Icon

You may want to create a **shortcut icon** that starts an application and opens a specific document file. To do this, simply create a shortcut icon for the document.

⁙ Saving Files

Option Buttons
Option buttons are sets of mutually exclusive choices. Option buttons are also called "radio buttons."

You can easily identify an option button set because it's a group of round buttons with a border. This is the **dialog box** that WordPad displays when you choose the View Options command. It uses the Word Wrap option button set to ask whether you want WordPad's **word wrap** feature turned on.

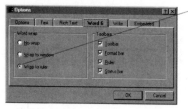

The selected option button shows a dot—called a "bullet"—in its center.

To select one of the option buttons in a set, you click the button.

You can also use the keyboard. For example, you can use the Tab key to select a button. Or you can press the Up and Down arrow keys to select a button. Or if the option buttons in a set show underlined letters, you can also select an option button by pressing the Alt key and the underlined letter. For example, you can select the No Wrap button in the preceding option button set by pressing Alt+N.

Overtyping   Normally, Windows-based **applications** insert the characters you type at the **insertion point.** By pressing the Ins (insert) key, however, you can often tell Windows-based applications to replace, or overtype, characters that follow the insertion point. Any text you type replaces existing text, starting with the character just to the right of the insertion point. To turn off overtyping, press the Ins key again.

Paint   The Paint **application** lets you create, print, store, and manipulate **bit map** images. To open Paint, click the **Start button.** Then choose Programs, Accessories, and Paint.

Creating a Bit Map Image

Once you start Paint, you use Paint tools to draw the lines and shapes and to add the colors that constitute the image.

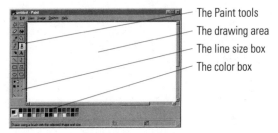

— The Paint tools
— The drawing area
— The line size box
— The color box

continues

Paint *(continued)*

Using the Paint Tools

To create bit map images, you use the Paint tools.

Tool	Description
	Use the *Free-Form Select* tool to draw a line (by dragging the mouse) around the image fragment you want to cut or copy. Then use the Edit Copy, Edit Cut, and Edit Paste commands to move the image fragment to and from the **Clipboard.**
	Use the *Select* tool to draw a box (by dragging the mouse diagonally between the box's opposite corners) around the image fragment you want to cut or copy. Then use the Edit Copy, Edit Cut, and Edit Paste commands to move the image fragment to and from the Clipboard.
	Use the *Eraser* tool to erase (by dragging the mouse) a portion of the image.
	Use the *Fill With Color* tool to color a shape (such as a box, a circle, or a polygon) or an image background. To color some shape or background, click the new color, click the tool, and then click the shape or background.
	Use the *Pick Color* tool to select a color from the color box. This sounds backward, I know. But suppose you can't quite tell which color green you've used. In this case, click the Pick Color tool. Then click a color in the image. Paint selects the color you picked from the color box.
	Use the *Magnifier* tool to magnify your view of the image so that you can actually see the pixels, or dots, of the color. To undo the magnification of the image, click the Magnifier tool and the drawing area again.
	Use the *Pencil* tool to draw (by dragging the mouse) a thin line in the selected color.
	Use the *Brush* tool to paint swaths of the selected color. To select the color, click one of the color boxes. To select the thickness of the brushstroke, click one of the line size boxes in the bottom left corner of the **application window.**
	Use the *Airbrush* tool to spray (by dragging the mouse) the selected color on the image. To select the spray color, click one of the color boxes at the bottom of the Paint application window. To select the spray thickness, click one of the line size boxes in the bottom left corner of the application window.

Tool	Description
A	Use the *Text* tool to add text to an image. To add text, first draw a box (by dragging the mouse between the box's opposite corners), and then enter the text in the box (by typing). To select the text color, click one of the color boxes. (Use the Text menu commands to control other features of the text.)
****	Use the *Line* tool to draw (by dragging the mouse) a line of the selected color and thickness. Use the color and line size boxes to specify the color and thickness.
?	Use the *Curve* tool to draw a curved line of the selected color. To use this tool, first draw a straight line by dragging the mouse. Then curve the line by dragging it. To select the color, click one of the color boxes. To select the thickness of the line, click one of the line size boxes.
▭	Use the *Rectangle* tool to draw a box (by dragging the mouse between the box's opposite corners). Use the color and line size boxes to specify the box's border line color and thickness.
◩	Use the *Polygon* tool to draw a shape using a series of lines. To draw the lines, click the line endpoints.
○	Use the *Ellipse* tool to draw circles and ovals (by dragging the mouse along the radius) of the selected color and using a line of the selected thickness.
▢	Use the *Rounded Rectangle* tool to draw a rectangle that has rounded corners. This tool, as you no doubt guessed, works like the Rectangle tool described earlier.

Drawing Squares and Circles

To draw a square with one of the box tools or a circle with one of the circle or ellipse tools, hold down the Shift key as you drag the mouse.

Printing an Image

Choose the File Print command to print the image. Graphic images are time-consuming to print, by the way. You may want to go get a cup of coffee.

Saving and Retrieving Images

You save your images on a disk and also retrieve them from the disk in the same way as you do any other file. Go figure.

 **Opening Files; Saving Files**

Paintbrush The Paintbrush **application** doesn't exist anymore. Windows 95 replaces Paintbrush with **Paint.**

Phone Dialer Windows 95 provides a telephone dialer **application.** If you use the same telephone line for both your **modem** and your phone, you can use Phone Dialer to dial numbers. (With this setup, probably your modem plugs into your wall telephone outlet and your telephone plugs into your modem.)

To use Phone Dialer, click the Start button. Then choose Programs, **Accessories,** and Phone Dialer.

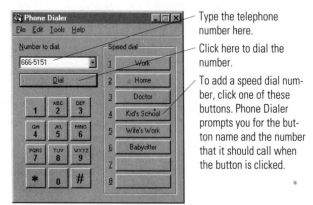

Type the telephone number here.

Click here to dial the number.

To add a speed dial number, click one of these buttons. Phone Dialer prompts you for the button name and the number that it should call when the button is clicked.

PIF PIFs describe how MS-DOS **applications** are supposed to run under Windows 95 in their own little **virtual machines.** If you know what you're doing, you can create and modify a PIF by setting **properties** for an individual MS-DOS session. If at this point you're saying, "What the heck?", don't worry. PIFs are way beyond the scope of our little book and are not generally of concern to most users.

Plug and Play The term "plug and play" simply means that you don't have to do anything fancy to get some new-fangled piece of computer gear working. You won't, as I once did, spend an entire Memorial Day weekend trying to get a bunch of **multimedia** gear installed and working. You just plug in the new gear (that is, connect it to your computer) and then use it. Windows 95 now provides and works with a bunch of system information in an effort to make plug and play not only a great concept but a reality. Alas, however, it'll be some time before everything is truly plug and play.

Pointer The pointer is the arrow that moves across your screen as you roll the mouse across your desk.

Oh oh. What's that? You don't have a mouse? OK. If you have some other kind of pointing device, such as a trackball, the pointer is the arrow that moves across your screen as you noodle around with this other, unidentified pointing device.

I should also mention that Windows-based **applications** change what the pointer looks like as a secret signal to you about what they're doing. If a Windows-based application is busily working at some time-consuming task, for example, the pointer may look like a tiny hourglass.

Points One point equals 1/72 inch. In Windows 95, you often specify sizes in points. **Fonts,** for example, get sized this way.

Pop-Up Box A pop-up box looks like a **message box,** but it doesn't have a **title bar,** and it doesn't have a Control menu. **Help** uses pop-up boxes to display its **help glossary** definitions. **Character Map** uses pop-up boxes to display an enlarged picture of the selected character symbol.

PostScript PostScript is the other scalable font technology, besides **TrueType.** PostScript is popular with desktop pub-
lishers and graphic designers. (We use PostScript fonts,
for example, to do the desktop publishing for this and the
other Field Guides.)

Unfortunately, most people encounter two practical problems with PostScript: PostScript fonts are expensive, and
printing PostScript documents is slow.

Printers In Windows 95, you don't need to describe your printer
or printers every time you install a new **application.** You
need to describe a printer only once.

Describing a New Printer

You can describe which printers you will use with Windows 95 by
using the Printers settings. To do this, follow these steps:

1   Click the **Start button.** Next choose Settings and then Printers to
display the Printers window.

2   Double-click the Add Printer icon. Windows 95 displays the first
Add Printer Wizard dialog box. There's nothing much on this dialog
box except the Next button, so I don't show it here.

3   Click Next. Windows 95 displays the second Add Printer Wizard
dialog box. It asks whether you're installing a local printer (that is,
one connected to your computer) or a network printer (one connected to another computer).

4 Click the Local printer option button, and then click Next. In the third Add Printer Wizard dialog box, Windows 95 asks for the printer manufacturer and printer model.

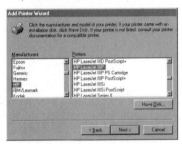

5 Select the printer manufacturer from the Manufacturers list box on the left.

6 Select the printer model from the Printers list box on the right.

7 Click Next. Windows 95 displays the fourth Add Printer Wizard dialog box to ask which port, or socket, your printer cable connects to.

8 Select the printer port. It'll probably be LPT1. If you're really stuck, take a look at the back of your computer. There's a good chance the ports are labeled ("LPT1," "LPT2," and so on).

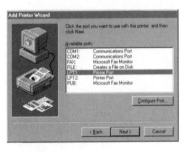

9 Click Next. Windows 95 displays the fifth Add Printer Wizard dialog box. It asks you to name the printer. Go ahead if you want. But you don't have to do this. You can just accept Windows 95's suggestion.

10 Click Next. Windows 95 displays the sixth Add Printer Wizard dialog box. Ugh. It asks if it's all right to print a test page. Go ahead. Just do it. All you need to do is click Finish.

continues

Printers *(continued)*

A slight detour

It's likely that after you've clicked Finish in step 10, Windows 95 will want you to find one of the original installation disks and plop it into your floppy disk drive. Windows 95 will ask this of you if it needs more information about the printer than it already has. Don't worry if this happens, by the way. All you need to do is find the disk and insert it.

Changing the Active Printer

If you install more than one printer, you can change which printer Windows 95 uses. To do so, display the Printers window (such as by clicking the Start button, choosing Settings, and then choosing Printers). Then select the printer (such as by clicking it), and choose the File Set As Default command.

 This, by the way, is the Printers window.

Changing the way a printer works

You can change the way a printer works by selecting the printer in the Printers window and then choosing the File Properties command. Windows 95 displays a dialog box that includes a bunch of tabs that let you make whatever changes the printer allows.

Printing When you tell an **application** to print some **document,** the application actually creates a printable copy of the document (called a "spool file") and then sends this printable copy to Windows 95. Windows 95 then prints the document.

In case you're interested, Print Manager for earlier versions of Windows doesn't exist anymore. All that printing stuff has been rolled into Windows 95 itself.

Print Queue The print queue is simply the list of **documents** (called "print spool files") that Windows 95 is printing or is supposed to be printing. This sounds funny. But let me give you the lowdown. Windows 95 collects the printable copies of documents that various **applications** send it, lines them up in a queue, and then prints these documents one at a time.

Viewing the Queue

To view the print queue, display the Printers window by clicking the Start button, choosing Settings, and then choosing Printers. Next select the printer whose queue you want to view, and choose the File Open command.

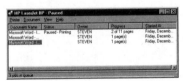

The printer window lists the documents, or spool files, that a specific printer is busily printing.

Canceling a Printing Document

To tell Windows 95 that it shouldn't print one of the documents listed in the print queue, select the document name and then choose the Document Cancel Printing command.

continues

Print Queue *(continued)*

Stopping and Starting Printing

You can use the Printer Pause Printing command to stop and start the printer. You can also use the Document Pause Printing command to stop and start the printing of the selected document. The commands work like a toggle switch. When printing is paused, there's a checkmark by the command name.

Deferred printing

Even if your computer isn't physically connected to a printer, you can still choose the File Print command in applications. Windows 95 simply creates a spool file, stores it in a print queue, and then waits until you do connect your computer to a printer. This is very handy, by the way. It means, for example, that you could do a bunch of work at home on your **laptop computer**, print all the stuff you wanted, and then just reconnect your laptop once you got to the office.

Program Items In earlier versions of Windows, program items were the icons that represented the applications in a **group.** Windows 95 doesn't have program items. Windows 95 does have a related icon, however: the **shortcut icon.**

Program Manager In earlier versions of Windows, you typically used Program Manager to start applications. Windows 95 provides a replacement for Program Manager: the powerful **Windows Explorer** application. Windows 95 also has a **shell**—double-click the My Computer icon to see it—that some people think closely resembles Program Manager. You can still use Program Manager if you really want to.

> **Troubleshooting: You Want to Use a Windows 3.0, 3.1, or 3.11 Application**

Properties If you want to change the way your computer works or the way something connected to your computer works, you change its properties. To do this, you **right-click** the **icon** that represents your computer or the thing you're trying to change. Then, when Windows 95 displays a **shortcut menu,** you choose the Properties command. Windows 95 displays a Properties dialog box, called a "property sheet." It includes a bunch of **tabs** that let you change stuff about whatever you clicked in the first place.

I don't describe properties in painstaking detail in this little book. For most people and most computers, the initial property settings are fine. No. Let me restate that more forcefully: For most situations, the initial property settings are best. That much said, however, know that you can noodle around on your own. Windows 95 prevents you from getting into too much trouble.

One warning: Don't ever change a property setting if Windows 95 warns you that the setting should be adjusted only by experienced users or system administrators—unless you really know what you're doing.

Protocol In the world of diplomacy, "protocol" refers to the rules of etiquette and ceremony that diplomats and heads of state follow. For example, "Don't drink from your finger bowl."

In the world of computers, "protocol" refers to the rules that two computers use to communicate. For example, "Don't send me data faster than I can receive it."

 HyperTerminal

Quick View If you're looking through the **files** in a **folder** using **Windows Explorer** or My Computer, you can look at the files without actually opening them. This quick look-and-see is called a "quick view." To quick view a file, select it. Then choose the File Quick View command.

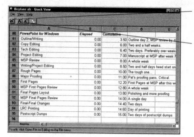

Click here to open the file you're quick viewing.

Use this button to magnify the size of what's shown in the window.

Radio Buttons ⁘ **Option Buttons**

README Files Software developers (such as Microsoft and Lotus Development) and hardware manufacturers (such as IBM or Compaq) often put late-breaking information in **WordPad** or **Notepad** files. Then they create **shortcut icons** (usually named something like "Read Me") that start WordPad or Notepad and load the file with the late-breaking information.

Recycle Bin When you **erase files, Windows Explorer** doesn't always remove the files from your disk. If you're erasing files from a **hard disk,** Windows Explorer moves the files to a special type of **folder** called the Recycle Bin. It does this so that you can later restore the files if necessary.

If you want to see which files are in the Recycle Bin, you can double-click the Recycle Bin **shortcut icon,** which appears on the desktop. You can also use Windows Explorer to display the Recycle Bin's contents in the folder pane.

This is the Recycle Bin.

Click these buttons to sort deleted files by name, original location, deletion date, type, and size. Click once, and Windows 95 sorts files in ascending order. Click again, and Windows 95 sorts files in descending order.

Undeleting Files

To recycle, or undelete, a file, follow these steps:

1 Select the file or files you want to undelete.

2 Choose the File Restore command.

Emptying the Recycle Bin

To empty the Recycle Bin—which is the same thing as really deleting the files—choose the File Empty Recycle Bin command.

continues

Recycle Bin *(continued)*

Controlling How the Recycle Bin Works

Windows 95 reserves up to a set percentage of your hard disk's space for storing files in Recycle Bin. Until you fill up the Recycle Bin, Windows 95 just adds deleted files to the Recycle Bin. When the Recycle Bin is full, Windows 95 still adds just-deleted files to the Recycle Bin, but to make room it removes the oldest file or files.

You can turn off the file recycling feature by right-clicking the Recycle Bin shortcut icon and choosing the Properties command. (If you're working with Windows Explorer, you can also **right-click** the Recycle Bin folder.)

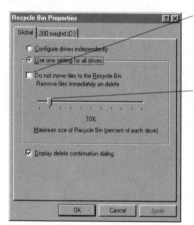

Click this check box if you don't want deleted files moved to the Recycle Bin—if you want them deleted instantly instead.

Use this **slide control** to set the Recycle Bin size as a percent of disk space.

Regional Settings You can customize Windows 95 so that it uses the appropriate language and the appropriate currency symbol and formats dates and times the way you want. To make these sorts of adjustments, click the **Start button.** Next choose Settings and then **Control Panel.** Then double-click the Regional Settings tool.

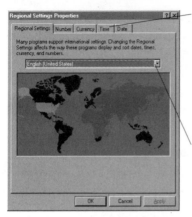

To make specific changes in the way that numbers are punctuated, currency amounts are displayed, and times and dates are displayed, click the appropriate **tab.** Then use its options to make your specifications.

Select an entry from the drop-down list box to change the Date, Time, Currency, and Number formats all in one fell swoop.

Registry Windows 95 keeps descriptions of all the stuff connected to your computer. These descriptions are stored in something called the "registry." You may not think that this is all that neat. But it is. Why? Because with Windows 95 keeping track of all this stuff, you don't have to.

Registry vs. WIN.INI and SYSTEM.INI

The Windows 95 registry pretty much replaces the initialization files used in the earlier versions of Windows. Windows 95 doesn't need any initialization files. Neither do Windows 95 applications. For backward compatibility, however, Windows 95 does allow the old initialization files to stick around. ("Stick around," by the way, is my favorite Arnold Schwarzenegger line. It's from the movie classic "Commando.")

Remote Access If you've got a **laptop computer** at home or on the road, you can use a Windows 95 feature called "Dial-Up Networking" to connect to your computer back at the office or to any other network. If you think you want to do this, ask your system administrator for instructions.

Renaming Files
Use **Windows Explorer** to rename files. To start Windows Explorer, click the **Start button.** Next choose Programs and then Windows Explorer.

Renaming a File
To rename a file once you've started Windows Explorer, follow these steps:

1 Click the disk drive icon of the disk that contains the file.

2 Click the **folder** that contains the file.

3 Select the file.

4 Click the file name. Or choose the File Rename command.
   To show that you can rename the file, Windows Explorer draws a box around the file name.

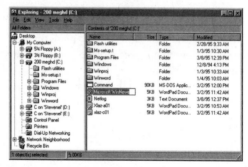

5 Type a new name for the file.

File Names

Right-Click
Usually, when you **click** the mouse, you click the left button. Because you mostly click the left button, I call this a "click" and not a "left-click." Sometimes, you do click the mouse's right button. But I can't call this a "click" without confusing you (and myself). So I call it a "right-click."

Unfortunately, there's a fly in the ointment about all this clicking business. Windows 95 lets you flip-flop the way the left and right mouse buttons work. And if you do so, your left mouse button will work in the way that I've said your right mouse button works, and your right mouse button will work in the way that I've said your left button works. But I find this extra complexity so confusing I just can't bear to write about it. So I'm going to stick with "click" and "right-click." (If you want to let out a low, almost subhuman scream at this point, go ahead. I really don't think it'll bother anyone nearby.)

By the way, you can right-click an **object** to display a **shortcut menu**. You might do this, for example, to change the **properties** of an object.

Root Directory Under MS-DOS, the root directory was the main directory that organized a hard disk's directories and those files that you didn't usually place in another directory. If your hard disk drive is named C, for example, you could see the root directory's directories and files by typing *dir c:* at the MS-DOS prompt.

Windows 95 doesn't have a root directory. You can start **Windows Explorer** and double-click the disk drive icon to see what **folders** and **files** it holds.

Saving Files You can almost always save the **document,** or file, that an **application** creates. For example, you can save the workbooks that Microsoft Excel creates, the documents that WordPerfect creates, the presentations that PowerPoint creates, and, well, you get the picture, right?

In general, you save the stuff shown in an **application window** or in an application window's **document windows** using the File Save As and File Save commands.

continues

Saving Files *(continued)*

Saving a File for the First Time

To save a file on a disk for the first time, you follow these general steps:

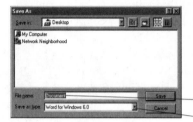

1 Choose the File Save As command. The application displays a **dialog box** named something like "Save As."

2 Enter a **file name.**

3 Use the **drop-down list boxes** to specify where the file should be located and the file type.

4 Click Save.

Saving a File Using a New Name or in a New Location

To save a file using a new name or in a new location, use the File Save As command as described in the preceding steps. Remember to specify the new name or location.

Resaving a File

To save a modified version of a file you've already saved before, you choose the File Save command. When you do this, the application replaces the original, saved-on-disk file with what is in memory and displayed on your screen.

ScanDisk ScanDisk is an **application** that looks through the **folders** and **files** on a disk drive, tracking down any errors. It's easy to use. Click the **Start button**. Then choose Programs, **Accessories,** System Tools, and ScanDisk.

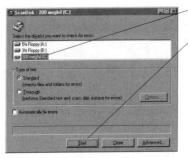

Click the disk drive you want to scan.

Click the Start button to scan. If ScanDisk encounters any errors, it displays a **dialog box** that lets you tell ScanDisk whether it should correct or ignore the errors.

Screen Saver A screen saver continually changes the picture shown on your screen so that an image isn't permanently etched into your screen by being displayed too long. I mention this because Windows 95 comes with a screen saver, which you turn on using **Control Panel's** Display tool.

To get to the Display tool, click the **Start button**. Then choose Settings and Control Panel. In Control Panel, double-click the Display icon. Finally, click the Screen Saver **tab.**

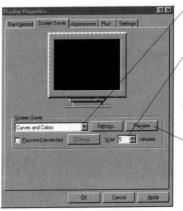

Use this **drop-down list box** to select a screen saver pattern.

Use the Wait **text box** to specify how long a period after keyboard or mouse inactivity the screen saver should be turned on.

To see what your screen saver looks like on the full screen, click the Preview button.

continues

115

Screen Saver *(continued)*

Once you've turned on the screen saver, Windows 95 displays the image after the specified period of inactivity. To remove the screen saver and see the Windows 95 **desktop** again, just move the mouse pointer or use the keyboard.

Assigning a Password

If you click the Password Protected **check box** and click the Change command button, Windows 95 lets you add a password that it requires before it will turn off the screen saver and redisplay the desktop. You might use a password to protect confidential information.

Wallpaper

Scroll Bars
Scroll bars let you move a document window's contents up and down and left and right. You do this, of course, because the document is too long or too wide to fit entirely within its window.

Using the Mouse to Scroll

You can use the mouse on a scroll bar in a couple of ways:

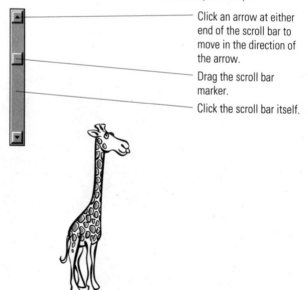

Click an arrow at either end of the scroll bar to move in the direction of the arrow.

Drag the scroll bar marker.

Click the scroll bar itself.

Scrolling Scrolling simply refers to paging through a **document**. You can use the vertical or horizontal **scroll bars** if you've got a mouse. You can also use the PgUp and PgDn keys to scroll vertically, and you can press Ctrl+PgUp and Ctrl+PgDn to scroll horizontally.

Selecting To change the contents of a **text box, list box,** or **combo box** or the setting of an **option button** or **check box,** you first need to select it. The easiest way to do this is by clicking the mouse. (In fact, if you don't have one, your next best investment in computer hardware is a mouse.)

You can also select a box or a button in the active **dialog box** by pressing the Alt key and the underlined letter.

Selecting Text Box Contents

To select chunks of text in text boxes—including single characters— click in front of the first character, and then drag the mouse to the space immediately following the last character.

Selection Cursor The selection cursor is the thing that marks the selected option in a **dialog box** or the selected text in a text box. OK. I know "thing" isn't a very specific noun. But how Windows 95 marks objects using the selection cursor depends on the object being marked.

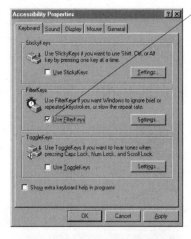

To mark a **check box** as selected, Windows 95 draws a line around the check box.

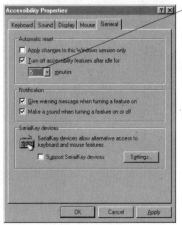

To mark a **text box, list box,** or **combo box's** contents as selected, Windows 95 highlights the text.

Insertion Point

Sharing Data Between Applications

You can easily share data between Windows-based **applications.** You can move worksheets and charts you've created in Microsoft Excel or Lotus 1-2-3, for example, to a word processor such as Microsoft Word or WordPerfect. You can move values and chunks of text between other Windows-based applications—for example, from **Calculator** to an accounting application.

To share data between applications, you follow these general steps:

1 Select what you want to share: a worksheet range, a chart, a chunk of text, a value, or anything else.

2 Choose the application's Edit Copy command to place the data on the **Clipboard**.

3 Switch to the other application by clicking its **task button**.

4 Position the **insertion point** where you want to place the copied data.

5 Paste the contents of the Clipboard at the insertion point location. (You'll probably do so using that application's Edit Paste or Edit Paste Special command.)

To link or to embed—that is the question

When you choose Edit Paste Special to paste an object—a worksheet fragment, for example—into another application's **document,** you can usually choose whether you want the pasted object to be linked to the source document or to be merely an embedded copy of the source document.

❖ **Drag-and-Drop; OLE; Switching Tasks**

119

Shell   Windows 95 doesn't need **Program Manager** anymore.
Windows Explorer and the **Start button,** for the most
part, do everything that Program Manager did and everything that **File Manager** did as well.

Windows 95 does, however, provide a shell, **My
Computer.** Like Program Manager, My Computer groups
applications and **files** (as well as a bunch of other stuff)
into **folders,** using windows to show the contents of these
folders. To use the shell, double-click the My Computer
icon on the **desktop.** When you do, the shell displays the
My Computer window, with icons that represent the stuff
you've got on or connected to your computer.

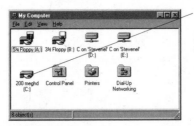

If you double-click this
icon, My Computer opens
another window that
shows the folders and
files on the hard disk.

   **Quick Reference: Windows Explorer and My Computer
Menu Guide**

Shortcut Buttons Shortcut buttons are clickable buttons that
appear inside the text you read in a Help window. They
let you jump quickly to other screens of help information
and to dialog boxes described in the help text.

  Help

Shortcut Icons Windows 95 lets you add icons for commonly
used **documents, applications, folders** (and other stuff
like this) to the **desktop.** This maybe doesn't seem like all
that neat a deal, but it is. If these icons are displayed on
the desktop, you can open a document, application, or
folder simply by double-clicking an icon.

S

Shortcut to
Field Guide

This is a shortcut icon.
Windows 95 uses an icon
that identifies the
application it'll instruct to
open the document—in
this case, Microsoft
Word.

Creating a Shortcut Icon

To create a shortcut icon for a document, or file, follow these steps:

1 Display **Windows Explorer** by clicking the Start button and then choosing Programs and Windows Explorer.

2 Select the document for which the shortcut icon should be created. (You may need to first select the folder that holds the document.)

3 Choose the File Create Shortcut command. Windows Explorer adds a shortcut icon to the folder.

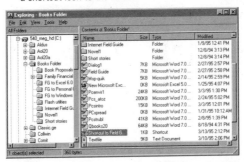

4 Drag the shortcut icon to the desktop. Windows Explorer then moves the shortcut icon to the desktop.

continues

121

Shortcut Icons *(continued)*

Deleting a Shortcut Icon
To delete a shortcut icon, click it, and then press Del.

Renaming a Shortcut Icon
To rename a shortcut icon, **right-click** it, choose the Rename command from the **shortcut menu,** and then type the new name.

Let's get technical about shortcut icons

Most of the shortcut icons you create will be for documents. Maybe you'll even create a few for applications, too. But while these may be the common uses of shortcut icons, they aren't the only uses. You can create shortcut icons for Control Panel tools, disks, and folders, thereby creating an easy way to open one of these thingamajigs. You can also add shortcut icons (for any of the objects I've discussed here) to files, thereby creating an easy way for someone to get access to a file you want to share. One other thing. Inasmuch as I've now used the word "thereby" in two consecutive sentences, I promise not to use the word for the rest of the book. Happy?

Shortcut Menus
A cool new feature you're seeing in many Windows-based applications is the shortcut menu—also known as the "context menu." Here's the scoop in case you don't already know. Many applications are now smart enough to know which commands make sense in which situations. Many applications also know which commands you, as a user, are most likely to use in those situations. If you want them to, many applications will display a shortcut menu that shows only these commands. To display the shortcut menu, **right-click** on the object you want to manipulate.

Changing Properties
If you point to some object on the screen and right-click, you'll almost always see a Properties command on a shortcut menu. You can use this command to change the properties of the object you clicked.

Shut Down ❖ Exiting Windows 95

Slide Control A slide control is just a type of scroll bar marker that, if dragged, doesn't scroll the contents of a document window. Instead, dragging the slide control tells a Windows-based application to adjust some setting or value.

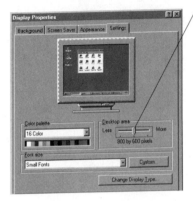

Adjusting this slide control changes the resolution of your desktop display. (You can display this **dialog box** on your screen by right-clicking the desktop, choosing the Properties command, and then clicking the Settings tab.)

❖ Scroll Bars

SmartDrive SmartDrive, which was the old MS-DOS **disk-caching** application, doesn't exist anymore in Windows 95. Windows 95 has something even better—the 32-bit **VCACHE.**

Sound Recorder You use the Windows Sound Recorder **application** to play, record, and edit sound files. If you want to use this application, though, you'll need to have the appropriate sound hardware device, and you'll need to have it installed.

To use Sound Recorder, click the Start button. Then choose Programs, Accessories, Multimedia, and Sound Recorder.

❖ Opening Files

Start Button

The Start button appears at the left end of the Taskbar. You use the Start button to start **applications,** to **open files,** to get to **Control Panel,** and even to exit from, or shut down, Windows 95. To press the Start button, you can click it. Or you can simultaneously press the Ctrl and Esc keys.

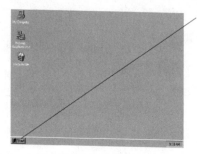

This, as you've no doubt guessed, is the Start button.

Starting Windows 95

You start Windows 95 by turning on your computer. After a second or two, you'll see a message at the top of your screen, "Starting Windows 95." The suspense begins to build at this point, of course. After a few seconds, you'll see the Windows 95 copyright notice screen. After a few more seconds, you'll see the Windows 95 **desktop.**

If, for some reason, you don't want Windows 95 to start when you start your computer, you can press F8 when you see the "Starting Windows 95" message. This tells Windows 95 to display the Windows 95 Startup menu, which gives you a bunch of different choices for starting your computer, including options to instead start MS-DOS in a handful of different ways.

Starting Windows-Based Applications
You start a Windows-based **application** either by opening a **document,** or **file,** created by the application or by opening the application itself.

Starting an Application by Opening a Document

To start an application by opening a document, follow these steps:

1 Start Windows Explorer by clicking the **Start button** and then choosing Programs and Windows Explorer.

2 Display the **folder** that includes the document, or file.

3 Double-click the document, or file.

About the Documents Submenu

The Documents **submenu** lists up to the last fifteen documents you've used. If you see the document you want on this menu, you can open it by clicking it. To display the Documents submenu, click the Start button and then choose Documents.

Starting an Application Directly

To start an application without opening a document, click the Start button and then choose Programs. Next, choose the submenu that contains the application. Finally, choose the application from the submenu.

Start Menu
The Start menu is what gets displayed when you click the **Start button.** You can add items to the Start menu and also add and remove items from one of the Start menu's submenus—the Programs menu.

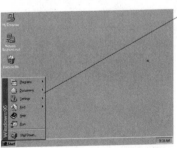

This is the Start menu.

continues

125

S

WINDOWS 95 A TO Z

Start Menu *(continued)*

Adding Items to the Start Menu or Program Menu

First, create a **shortcut icon** for the item you want to add, as described in that entry. Second, click the Start button. Last, choose Settings and Taskbar to display the Taskbar Properties dialog box, click the Start Menu Programs tab, and then click the Advanced button. Initially, you see only the Programs icon in the Start Menu window.

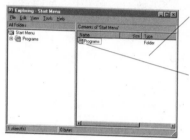

To add a shortcut icon to the Start menu, drag it from the desktop to this window.

To add a shortcut icon to the Programs menu, click here to see the Programs menu's submenus. Then drag the shortcut icon from the desktop to this window.

Removing Items on the Programs Menu

You can remove items on the Programs menu and on any of its **submenus,** too. To do this, display the Taskbar Properties dialog box as described in the preceding paragraph. Then click the Remove button. Windows 95 then opens a window of the items that are on that menu. (To work with a submenu, you could click that submenu's icon.)

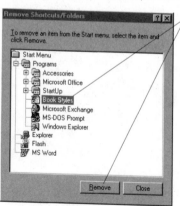

To remove an item from the Programs menu or from one of its submenus, click the item and then click Remove.

Starting Windows-Based Applications

Startup Menu No. This isn't an error. In addition to the **Start menu** just described, there's also a Startup menu. It lists any **applications** you want started and any **documents** you want opened when Windows 95 starts.

You can add applications and documents to the Startup menu in the same way that you add items to other menus—including the Start menu. Since I just described how you do this, I won't repeat myself here. Instead, just read the preceding entry. (The Startup menu is a **submenu** that appears on the Programs submenu of the Start menu.)

One other thing. As you strive to keep all this madness straight, don't confuse the Startup menu I've mentioned here with the Microsoft Windows 95 Startup menu, which is what appears if you press F8 to start MS-DOS rather than Windows 95 when you start your computer. That menu is something different.

꙳ **Booting Using MS-DOS**

Subfolder I use the term "subfolder" to refer to a **folder** within a folder. This isn't some technical term I learned over at Microsoft, by the way. I just made it up.

Submenu I use the term "submenu" to refer to a **menu** that appears when you choose another menu. This term I didn't make up. Computer trade book writers have used the term "submenu" ever since, well, ever since the first computer trade book writer crawled out of the primordial ooze.

Suspend When you choose the Shut Down command from the **Start menu,** you see a **dialog box** that asks, "Hey, what do you mean, 'shutdown'?" One of your options is Suspend. Basically, the Suspend option partially shuts down stuff on your computer to reduce its power usage. (This works only on computers that let you reduce their power usage.)

Switching Tasks In Windows 95, to switch from **application** to application, or **multitask,** you use the **Start button** and **Taskbar.** You use the Start button to start new applications. You use the Taskbar to switch between the applications you've already started.

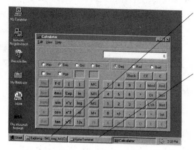

This is the Taskbar. The buttons you see represent each of the open applications.

To switch to this application, just click its button.

Tab   If there's too much stuff to fit in a **dialog box,** Windows 95 and Windows-based applications may separate options onto different pages, or what are called "tabs."

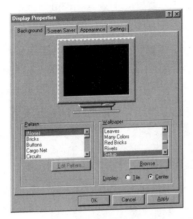

To move to the "page" of Settings options, click its tab.

Taskbar The Taskbar shows at the very bottom of your screen. It provides the **Start button** and buttons for any additional **applications** that Windows 95 or you have started.

You can use the Taskbar's **task buttons** to make another application the **foreground application.**

Oh. Let me tell you one other thing, too. You can move and resize the Taskbar by dragging it.

   ☙ **Background Applications; Switching Tasks**

Task Button Windows 95 shows buttons on the **Taskbar** for each **application** that you or Windows 95 starts. You can make an application the **foreground application** by clicking its button.

I don't know what else to call these buttons, so I'm going with "task buttons."

Terminal Terminal was the communications **application** for the earlier versions of Windows. You won't need or want to use Terminal anymore, however. You'll want to use **HyperTerminal** instead. HyperTerminal is much faster because it's a **32-bit** application.

Text Box A text box is simply an input blank you fill in by typing. To do this, select the text box (such as by clicking) and then start typing.

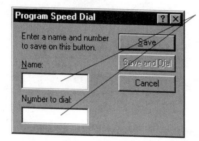

These input blanks, or boxes, are text boxes.

Deleting Characters in a Text Box

Position the **insertion point** by clicking or using the Left and Right arrow keys. Use the Backspace key to erase the character that precedes the insertion point; use the Del key to erase the character that follows the insertion point.

Replacing the Contents of a Text Box

Position the insertion point at the beginning of the text box by clicking. Drag the mouse to the last character of the text box to select the entire text box contents. Then type the replacement text. What you type replaces the selected text.

Threads This is sort of technical. But it's fun, too. Here's the story on threads. When you open an **application**—like your word processor, for example—Windows 95 starts what it calls a "process." This process, in turn, starts what are called "threads." One thread might look at what you type and enter it in a **document.** Another thread might do the work of printing a document in the background. Maybe another thread spell-checks the document. In effect, then, when you open an application, you start a whole bunch of miniature applications. (This isn't exactly right, but it's close enough for our purposes.)

Threads are cool because they let you do more work more quickly. Threads are also new to the world of Windows 95. An operating system needs to be smart enough to handle a bunch of these things. The earlier versions of Windows weren't, just for the record.

Preemptive multitasking makes it all possible

In case you're interested, what makes this threads business possible is that Windows 95 does what's called "preemptive multitasking." All this means is that if you do start more than one process and these processes start multiple threads, Windows 95 is smart enough to divvy up your computer's resources in a fair and orderly way. In comparison, the earlier versions of Windows did what was called "cooperative multitasking." In that environment, each of the applications you started had to, in effect, do the divvying up itself. If you had a poorly behaved application that was selfish about sharing, things got ugly fast.

Times ❖ **Dates and Times**

Title Bars

Title bars identify the **application** that's running in an application window and the **document** that's displayed in a document window.

The title bars of the active **application window** and active **document window** usually show in a color that is different from the color used for title bars in inactive windows. Using the default Windows 95 color palette, for example, the title bar of the active window is blue, and the inactive windows' title bars are gray.

❖ **Colors**

Toolbars

Toolbars are those rows of buttons and boxes, or tools, that sometimes appear at the top of your window just below the **menu bar.** Toolbar buttons provide shortcuts for common menu commands.

The MS-DOS window, which appears when you choose Programs and then MS-DOS Prompt from the Start menu, provides a toolbar.

TrueType

TrueType is Microsoft Corporation's scalable **font** technology. If you're working with a Windows-based application, using TrueType fonts in your documents delivers two benefits. First, Windows 95 and Windows-based applications come with some cool TrueType fonts. (OK. Maybe that shouldn't count as a benefit, but you don't get any **PostScript** fonts with Windows 95 or with Microsoft applications, which is the competitive scalable font product.) Second, because of the way a scalable font is created, it's easy for Windows 95 and Windows-based applications to change the point size in a way that results in legible fonts. Windows 95 identifies TrueType fonts in the various Font list boxes by using the **T̄r** prefix.

Adding Fonts

If you buy additional TrueType fonts, you can add them using Control Panel's Fonts tool. Open the Fonts folder by clicking it. Then use the File Install New Font Command.

VCACHE Windows 95 comes with a slick **disk-caching** application, VCACHE. (Let's pronounce it "Vee-cash".) VCACHE is cool for two reasons. One, it's a lot smarter than the old disk-caching application, SmartDrive. Two, it's **32-bit**. Three, it's dynamic about the way it gobbles **memory**. If you've got a lot of free memory, VCACHE uses a bunch of memory. If you don't, it doesn't. Oh, sorry. That's three reasons, isn't it?

⁘ Disk Caching

Virtual Machine A virtual machine is essentially a make-believe computer that Windows 95 creates whenever you start a copy of MS-DOS or any MS-DOS **application** from inside Windows 95. Because Windows 95 is a lot smarter than MS-DOS, MS-DOS and any MS-DOS application think the fake is the real McCoy and go on their merry way.

You don't really need to know this, but since you're already reading here I'll tell you that every time you start an MS-DOS application from inside Windows 95, it creates a new, separate virtual machine for that application. In theory, if you really knew your stuff, you could create a **PIF** file to configure, or tweak, each one of these virtual machines so that the PIF file described a computer exactly like the one the application wanted.

Virtual Memory Virtual memory simply refers to the disk
space a computer uses as **memory**. I mention this here
because Windows 95 uses virtual memory. Fortunately,
you don't have to do anything to get Windows 95 to do
the virtual memory thing. Windows 95 takes care of the
whole process all by itself.

For you technical types

You can control how Windows 95 deals with virtual memory. To do this, display
the System Properties dialog box by right-clicking the My Computer icon on the
desktop, choosing Properties, and then clicking the Performance **tab** to display
the performance options. Finally, click the Virtual Memory command button.
Windows 95 presents you with options that let you specify the size of a
permanent swapfile that Windows 95 will use for virtual memory. (The disk space
doing double-duty as memory is called a "swap file.") I have no idea why you
would want to do this, however. You won't get any improvement in performance
(or so the folks at Microsoft tell me). And you tie up a chunk of disk space.

 **Disk Caching; VCACHE**

Virus A "virus" is a program created by a pathetic little wimp
who has a bit of technical knowledge but zero maturity,
zero common sense, and zero morals. The virus program
this loser creates often attempts to destroy either your
computer or the data stored on your computer's hard
disk.

You get viruses by using infected **floppy disks** or infected
software with your computer. If you use only software
from reputable, professional software developers and you
don't carelessly share floppy disks with all your computer
friends, you don't have much to worry about when it
comes to viruses.

Wallpaper Windows 95 lets you change the desktop pattern or wallpaper—the area that appears behind the windows of Windows 95—using **Control Panel.**

Once you've displayed Control Panel (such as by clicking the **Start button** and choosing Settings and then Control Panel), double-click the Display tool. Control Panel displays a **dialog box** that includes options for changing the desktop wallpaper. (Click the Background **tab** if the dialog box isn't already showing.)

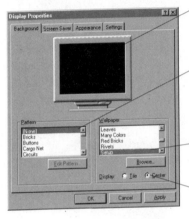

This picture of a monitor shows how your pattern and wallpaper choices look.

Select a pattern from this list box. There are a bunch of different choices. Go ahead and fool around a bit.

As an alternative to the pattern, use this **list box** to select a wallpaper.

If you pick a wallpaper, use these **option buttons** to specify how the wallpaper should be laid out, or "hung."

 Screen Saver

Wildcard Characters

Wildcard characters help you search for text strings and characters when you can't or don't want to be precise about all the characters in the name of what you're looking for. There are two wildcard characters you need to know: * (the asterisk) and ? (the question mark). The * takes the place of any number of characters. For example, if you wanted to find all file names that ended in ".TXT" (all text files, typically), you could specify this as *.*TXT*. This specification would find both FILE1.TXT and 1.TXT. The question mark, by contrast, takes the place of only 1 character. For example, if you wanted to find all files that used just 8 characters in their name and began with "text," you would use *TEXT????.** to specify this. This specification would find TEXT1126.DOC and TEXTBARB.TXT but not TEXT123.TXT.

Window Buttons

Arranged around the outside edge of the **application window** and **document windows** are buttons and icons. You can use these to display the **Control menu,** to close windows, and to minimize and change window size.

Button or Icon	Description
	Displays the Microsoft Word application's Control menu. (Different applications use different icons for their Control menus, as you might have guessed. This is the icon for Word.)
	Displays the document window's Control menu.
	Minimizes a window by turning it into a button.
	Restores a window to its previous size.
	Maximizes a window. Maximized application windows fill the screen. Maximized document windows fill the application window.
	Closes the window. Closing an application window, by the way, closes the application.

Window Panes

In some **applications,** you can split a **document window** into panes and then use the panes to view different portions of the same document. You might do this, for example, to view a word processor document's table of contents (from page 1) in one pane and a later section (from page 21) in another pane.

The way you create panes depends on the application, but the rules are fairly straightforward if you're working with a Microsoft application.

Creating Window Panes

Follow these steps to split a window into panes in a Microsoft application such as Microsoft Word or Microsoft Excel:

1 Choose the Window Split command to split the active document window into two panes. To show the split window, an application often displays a fuzzy, thick horizontal line through the middle of the document window.

2 Use the mouse or the Up and Down arrow keys to move this "pane-splitting" line to the place you want the window split.

3 Press Enter or click the mouse to anchor the line.

Removing Window Panes

To remove a window pane in a Microsoft application such as Word or Excel, choose the Window Remove Split command. (This command replaces the Window Split command once you've split a window into panes.)

Jumping Between Window Panes

You can move the **insertion point** between window panes by clicking one pane or the other.

Windows Explorer

Windows Explorer lets you do two things: It lets you view and work with your computer's disks and the files you've got stored on your disks. And it lets you view and work with the other parts of your computer—its **fonts, Control Panel,** and **printers.**

Starting Windows Explorer

To start Windows Explorer, click the **Start button.** Next, choose Programs and then Windows Explorer.

Windows Explorer uses a **folder pane** to show the **folder** structure.

Windows Explorer uses a **file pane** to show the **subfolders** and the files in the active folder. It provides information such as the file size in **kilobytes** and the date on which the file was last modified.

Selecting Disks

To select a disk, click the disk icon.

Selecting Folders

To select a folder, scroll through the folder pane until you see the folder you want. Then click the folder.

If the folder is a subfolder in another folder (the "parent folder"), you may need to first select the parent folder and display its subfolder. You can do this by clicking the parent folder.

Windows Explorer alerts you to subfolders

Windows Explorer places the plus sign (+) in front of a folder's icon if that folder has subfolders.

Selecting Files

To select a file in the active folder, scroll through the file pane until you see the file. Then click the file.

You can select multiple files by clicking the first file, holding down Shift, and then clicking the last file. Or you can also hold down Ctrl and then click each file.

Understanding Windows Explorer's Disk and File Icons

Windows Explorer uses different types of icons to represent folders and the various types of **documents,** or files. If you've come this far, you'll probably find it helpful to know what the different icons represent. Here is a list of the Windows Explorer icons:

Icon	Description
	Represents your **desktop.** If you click the desktop icon, Windows Explorer uses the file pane to show everything on your desktop—including any **shortcut icons.**
	Represents your computer, including its disks, printers, and any system folders for fonts and Control Panel settings.
	Represents a floppy disk drive. If you click the floppy disk drive icon, Windows Explorer uses the file pane to show the folders and files on the **floppy disk.**
	Represents a hard drive. If you click the hard drive icon, Windows Explorer uses the file pane to show the folders and files on the hard drive.
	Represents a folder. If the folder is active, the folder appears open. If the folder is inactive, the folder appears closed. If the folder holds subfolders, Windows Explorer places a plus sign (+) at the front of the folder.
	Represents an application file. You can start the application by double-clicking it or by selecting it and then choosing the File Open command. The various application file icons look different.
	Represents an associated document file. You can start the associated application and open this document file by double-clicking it or by selecting it and then choosing the File Open command. The exact appearance of an associated document file icon depends on the application it's associated with. Notice that the application icon—in this example, for Microsoft Word—appears in the upper left corner of the icon.

continues

139

Windows Explorer (continued)

Icon	Description
	Represents an unassociated document file. You can't open this document file by double-clicking. You can use the File Open With command to open this document file, but Windows Explorer asks you for the name of the application. (Windows Explorer changes the name of the command from File Open to File Open With if the selected document file isn't associated with an application.)
	Represents a CD-ROM drive. If you click the CD-ROM icon, Windows Explorer uses the file pane to show the folders and files that are on the CD.
	Represents your computer's fonts. If you click the fonts icon, Windows Explorer uses the file pane to show all the fonts installed on your computer.
	Represents Control Panel. If you click the Control Panel icon, Windows Explorer uses the file pane to show an icon for each of the Control Panel settings.
	Represents the **printers** available to your computer. If you click the printers icon, Windows Explorer uses the file pane to show icons for each of the installed printers.
	Represents the **network** your computer is attached to. If you click the Network Neighborhood icon, Windows Explorer uses the file pane to show the other computers, disks, folders, and files you can use because they're part of your network. (This works only if you are connected to a network.)
	Represents the **Recycle Bin.** If you click the Recycle Bin icon, Windows Explorer uses the file pane to show the files you've erased. You can unerase files in the Recycle Bin.
	Represents another computer that your computer can access remotely—or vice versa. If you click the Dial-Up Networking icon, Windows 95 sets itself up for **remote access.**
	Represents your **briefcase.** If you click the My Briefcase icon, Windows 95 synchronizes the files in your briefcase.

Copying Files; Erasing Files; Formatting Floppy Disks; Moving Files; Renaming Files; Troubleshooting: You Can't Find a File; You Accidentally Erased a File

Windows for Workgroups
Windows for Workgroups is another member of the Windows operating system family. What differentiates Windows for Workgroups from earlier versions of Windows is that Windows for Workgroups lets you connect personal computers in what's called a "peer-to-peer **network**" as long as each of the computers in the network runs Windows for Workgroups and has a special communications device called a "network card."

Are you now thinking, "Well, that sounds kind of cool; I wish Windows 95 did that?" Don't worry. Windows 95 does let you network.

 Windows NT

Windows NT
Windows NT is the most powerful version of the Windows operating system family; chances are you won't need it. With Windows NT, you get the same sorts of system security measures you do with a big computer system. And Windows NT lets your computer access monstrously huge chunks of memory (as much as 4 gigabytes) and even more monstrously huge chunks of disk space (as much as 137 gigabytes). Yikes.

 Windows: The Earlier Versions

Windows: The Earlier Versions
The predecessors to Windows 95—the earlier versions of Windows—were pretty cool operating environments. But they had some limitations. They were mostly **16-bit** operating systems, and that was sort of crummy. They didn't handle unruly and ill-mannered applications very well. And they weren't very fast.

Wizard If you look up the word "wizard" in the dictionary, it'll tell you that a wizard is someone skilled in magic. A sorcerer, if you will. That's kind of scary sounding, isn't it?

In Windows 95, wizards are different. Wizards help you accomplish complicated tasks more easily. Usually, they consist of a series of **dialog boxes** that ask you questions and provide lots of hand holding. In the entry that describes how you set up a **printer,** for example, I talk about one such wizard, the Add Printer Wizard. It makes configuring (another scary word) your computer easy. Windows 95 also provides wizards for setting up new devices and for using such things as **Remote Access.**

WordPad The WordPad **application** is a simple word processor. If you don't have another word processor, you should be able to use WordPad to do most of your writing, as long as the **documents** you want to produce aren't too complicated or fancy.

Starting WordPad

Start WordPad by clicking the **Start button** and then choosing Programs, **Accessories,** and WordPad.

Creating a Document

To enter text in a document, you simply use the keyboard to type the characters. Tap, tap, tap. No joke. That's all there is to it.

This is the Standard **toolbar.**

This is the Formatting toolbar.

To see what the toolbar's tools do, just position the mouse pointer over the button edge of the tool.

Don't press Return at the ends of lines; WordPad moves the **insertion point** to the next line when it runs out of room. WordPad also moves words from one line to the next line if there isn't room.

To edit text you've already entered, first select the character or block of text you want to change. (You can do this by clicking just before the first character you want to change and then dragging the mouse to just after the last character you want to change.) Next type the new text that will replace the old text.

You can erase the preceding character by pressing Backspace.

You can erase the current selection—a character, a sentence, a picture, or a paragraph—by pressing Del.

Editing Text

Use the Edit Undo command to undo, or reverse, the effect of your last editing operation.

Use the Edit Cut, Edit Copy, and Edit Paste commands to move and copy text. Use Edit Cut to move the selected text to the **Clipboard.** Use Edit Copy to make a copy of the selected text and place this copy on the Clipboard. Use Edit Paste to move whatever is on the Clipboard to your document. (The stuff gets placed wherever the insertion point is.)

Use the Edit Clear command to erase the selected text.

Use the Edit Select All command to select the entire document.

Use the Edit Find command to locate text in a document. When WordPad displays the Find **dialog box,** enter the text you're looking for in the text box. If you want to repeat the last Find search, use the Edit Find Next command.

Use the Edit Replace command to find text in a document and then replace it. When WordPad displays the Replace dialog box, enter the text you want to replace as well as the new replacement text.

continues

WordPad *(continued)*

Formatting a Document

One of the easiest ways to change the formatting of selected text is by using the Formatting toolbar. It provides a font drop-down **list box;** a font point size drop-down list box; tools for boldfacing, italicizing, underlining, and coloring text; and a bunch of other stuff as well. If you do something you don't like, click the tool again to undo your formatting. Or use the Edit Undo command.

Use the Format menu commands to change the **font,** add bullet points, modify paragraph formatting (alignment and indention), and noodle around with tabs.

I could probably write an entire chapter about doing this sort of formatting. Wait a minute. I *have* written entire chapters about formatting. But there isn't room in this little book. Go ahead. Experiment. You'll have more fun and learn the mechanics more quickly anyway.

Printing a WordPad Document

Choose the File Print command to print a WordPad document.

Saving a WordPad Document

To save your document on a disk, follow these steps:

1   Choose the File Save As command.

2   Type a file name for the document.

3   Use the list boxes to specify where the document file should be lo-
    cated.

4   Click Save.

Retrieving a WordPad Document

To retrieve a document you've previously stored on disk, start WordPad and then follow these steps:

1   Choose the File Open command.

2   Type the document's file name.

3   If necessary, use the list boxes to specify where the document is
    located.

4   Click Open.

Why get a word processor?

You're perhaps thinking to yourself, "WordPad comes with Windows 95. Hmmm. Why go out and spend good money on an expensive word processor?" Good question. In truth, you may not need to if you don't do much writing and if the documents you want to produce are pretty simple—letters home to Mom, say, or a quick memo every now and then. But you should know that an application such as Microsoft Word, WordPerfect, or Lotus AmiPro offers far more than does WordPad. All the real, live word processors are faster, do more, and do it better. And they also provide tools to make it easier to produce professional looking documents.

Opening Files; Saving Files

Word Wrap "Word wrap" simply means that a word processor such as WordPad or Notepad moves the **insertion point** to the next line once you run out of room on the current line and also moves big words to the next line if the move makes things fit better.

Write Earlier versions of Windows came with a simple word processor called Write. Now, however, this fact is of interest only to technology history buffs and to the mother of the programmer who wrote Write. Windows 95 replaces Write with something even better: **WordPad**.

Zmodem Zmodem is a file transfer protocol used by terminal applications like **HyperTerminal** to send files over telephone lines between your computer and other computers. A file transfer protocol allows different computers to send and receive files without corrupting those files. Zmodem got its name because it was developed to correct some of the limitations of its predecessors, Xmodem and Ymodem. Zmodem is generally considered to be one of the fastest and most reliable file transfer protocols. Many bulletin board systems (BBSs) support Zmodem.

TROUBLE-
SHOOTING

••

Got a problem? Starting on the next page are solutions to the problems that plague new users of Windows 95. You'll be on your way—and safely out of danger—in no time.

WINDOWS AND APPLICATIONS

You Can't Get an Application to Respond

It's unlikely but still possible that a bug in an **application** will cause it to stop responding, or, in the parlance of computer geeks, to "hang." If this happens, you won't be able to choose menu commands in that application. (You will still be able to choose menu commands in other applications, by the way.) And you may not be able to move the mouse pointer or click the mouse. (My experience is that the mouse pointer usually also looks like an hourglass or disappears completely.)

Try patience

It's possible that the application isn't actually unresponsive. It's possible that it's busy working on something you told it to do. Like saving the **document** on a disk. It's even possible that the application is busy working on something you didn't tell it to do. A word processor application might be busy breaking a long document into pages, for example.

For this reason, the first thing I'd try is a short break. Perhaps coffee and a cinnamon roll. I'm sure, too, that this strategy, which I've adopted as my own first defense, has nothing to do with my growing weight problem. It couldn't.

Terminate the hung application

Unfortunately, if an application truly is unresponsive—if it ignores your keyboard and mouse actions—there's nothing you can do to make it start responding again. When this is the case, however, you can press Ctrl+Alt+Del. (You'll have to find these three keys on your keyboard first, of course.)

Ctrl+Alt+Del—you press the three keys simultaneously—tell Windows 95 to look at each of the applications you've started, check for responsiveness, and display the Close Application dialog box.

Using the Close Application dialog box, Windows 95 identifies any unresponsive application as "not responding." To terminate an application, including one that is hung, select it and then click the End command button. To remove the Close Application dialog box, click the Close button.

You Get an Application Error

Sometimes an **application** asks Windows 95 to do the impossible. When this happens, Windows 95 displays a **message box** that says there's been an accident and that you had better come quick.

Close the application

When Windows 95 does alert you to an application error, it usually gives you two choices: Close and Details. You want to select Close. Details just gives you the gory specifics of what caused the application to go toes up.

It's also possible in rare cases for Windows 95 to give you the option of ignoring the error. Even in this case, the most prudent choice is still to close the application.

By the way, if you've been working with some **document** and have made changes you haven't yet saved, and you have the option of ignoring the error, you should ignore the application error and then save the document. Do save the document using a new **file name,** however. You don't want to replace the previous version of a document with a new, corrupted document. Then once you've saved the document, close the application.

You Want to Use a Windows 3.0, 3.1, or 3.11 Application

I've been working with Windows 95 for more than a year now. And I like the new way of doing things. I like **Windows Explorer** a lot better than the old **Program Manager** and **File Manager.** I like **HyperTerminal** much better than Terminal. I've also found the new parts of Windows 95 and the new accessory applications easy to learn. That much said, you still may have good reasons for wanting to use an old Windows application.

Use Windows Explorer to start the application

You can use Windows Explorer to start an application. You simply select the application and then choose the File Open command. To select the application, of course, you'll need to know that these applications are all in the Windows folder (which used to be the Windows directory), and you'll need to know the application's file name. (MS-DOS file names, which are what earlier versions of Windows use, are pretty cryptic, as you probably know.) Here's a list of the half dozen or so old Windows applications you may want to use:

Application	File name
Program Manager	PROGMAN.EXE
File Manager	WINFILE.EXE
Calendar	CALENDAR.EXE
Cardfile	CARDFILE.EXE
Clipboard Viewer	CLIPBRD.EXE
Clock	CLOCK.EXE
Paintbrush	PBRUSH.EXE
Terminal	TERMINAL.EXE

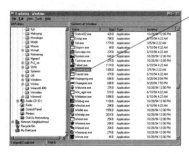

If several files have the same name, select the one that's identified as an application.

Create a shortcut icon for the application

You can create a shortcut icon for an old (earlier than Windows 95) Windows-based application, too. Start Windows Explorer, open the Windows folder, select the application, and then choose the File Create Shortcut command.

Add the application to the Start menu

You can also add old Windows applications to the Start menu or to one of its submenus, including the Startup menu. I described how to do this in the "Windows 95 A to Z" section of this Field Guide. So rather than repeat myself here, I'll just refer you there. Note, however, that you may need to know the application file names I just described a paragraph or so ago.

Installing Windows 3.1 applications

To install Windows 3.1 applications, use the Add/Remove Programs tool, which appears in the Control Panel folder. When you use this tool to install an application, the application is added to the Programs menu.

PRINTING

Your Printer Won't Print

A printer that won't print is usually easy to fix. Really. There are only a handful of things that may be wrong.

Verify the printer is on

Sounds silly, doesn't it? But go ahead and check this first.

Verify the printer is cabled correctly

There's a printer cable that connects your computer and printer. This is the conduit, or pipe, that your computer uses to send information to your printer. Make sure this cable is firmly plugged into both the computer and the printer.

Let me say something else, too. There's often more than one socket plug, or port, on the back of your computer into which the printer cable plugs. So you'll also want to make sure that you're plugging the printer cable into the correct port. Usually your printer cable plugs into the LPT1 port. (The port may even be labeled this way.)

Verify the printer is online

There should be an "online" light somewhere on the front of your printer, indicating that your printer is ready and willing to accept information from your computer. This light should be on. If it isn't, put the printer online. You usually do this by pressing an Online button or the Reset button. If you can't find either of these buttons on your printer, take a peek at the user guide that came with your printer.

Add the printer if you haven't already

In Windows 95, you need to add a new printer before you can use it. To add a new printer, you use a wizard. Thank goodness this is the case, too, because it makes everything really easy. All you have to do is open the Printers folder (such as by using **Windows Explorer**) and then double-click the Add Printer icon. Windows 95 starts the Add Printer Wizard and steps you through the process of describing your new printer. Don't worry, by the way. Windows 95 does most of the work for you. If you can read the manufacturer's name and the model name from the front of the printer, you're set.

Is your printer broken?

If none of the solutions described here work, it's very possible that your printer is broken. In this case, there's nothing you can do from inside Windows 95. If you've tried everything and failed, try to print a test page. You may also want to follow any troubleshooting directions described in the printer user guide. By doing these things, you'll be able to determine whether the printer is, in fact, broken. If it is, you'll need to take it to someone who repairs printers.

 Printing

You Want to Cancel a Printing Document

If you've told some application you want it to print a document that you later realize you don't need or want, you can cancel the printing of the document, particularly if the document is long or your printer is slow.

Cancel printing from within the application

If an application displays a message on the screen that says it's printing some document, you may be able to cancel the printing from within the application.

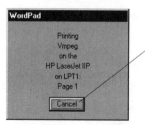

You can cancel the printing of this document just by clicking Cancel.

continues

153

You Want to Cancel a Printing Document *(continued)*

Cancel printing using Windows 95

When an application prints a document, what it really does is create a printable copy of the document and send this copy to Windows 95. Windows 95 then prints this printable copy—called a "spool file"—as well as any printable copies of documents that other applications have sent it. (Remember that you may be running more than one application, so it's possible that more than one application is sending spool files to Windows 95.)

To cancel printing using Windows 95, open the Printers **folder** by double-clicking it, and then double-click the icon for the printer to which you've been sending the spool files. Windows 95 then displays a **print queue** for the printer.

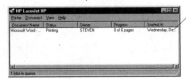

1 Select the printing document you want to cancel.

2 Choose the Document Cancel Printing command.

You Want to Postpone Printing a Document

If you've got a long **document** that you want to print eventually—but not quite yet—you can tell Windows 95 to cool its heels for that particular spool file.

Pause the printing of a document

To pause the printing of a particular document, open the Printers **folder** by double-clicking it, and then double-click the icon for the printer to which you've been sending the spool files. Windows 95 then displays a **print queue** for the printer.

1 Select the printing document you want to pause.

2 Choose the Document Pause Printing command.

When you want to print the document later, repeat this process. Choosing the Document Pause Printing command a second time will resume the printing.

Your Printer Stalls

Some documents—such as those that combine color and graphics—are very slow to print. This slowness, besides causing you irritation, can cause your printer problems. Windows 95 expects to be able to send your printer more data regularly (often every 45 seconds). If it takes 3 minutes to print a page, however, Windows 95 can't send the printer more information and might conclude that your printer isn't responding. Shortly after reaching this conclusion, Windows 95 will stop sending stuff to the printer. It may also display an on-screen message saying something like, "That printer of yours isn't responding again, and I'm pretty much at my wits' end."

Tell Windows 95 to retry

To tell Windows 95 to start printing again, display the printer folder window, and choose the Printer Pause Printing command. (To display the printer folder window, start **Windows Explorer,** open the Printers folder by clicking it, and then open the stalled printer by double-clicking it.) Or if Windows 95 displays a message box telling you that your darn printer has stalled, you can click the Retry command button if it appears in the message box. This might be all you need to do. Or if there are still several pages left in the presentation, you might need to sit in front of your computer and either choose the Printer Pause Printing command or click the Retry button a few more times.

continues

155

Your Printer Stalls *(continued)*

Increase the printer's Transmission Retry setting

If you're frequently getting the "Printer isn't responding" message or if you're going to be doing a lot of presentation printing, you might want to tell Windows 95 it's OK that your printer isn't quite as quick as Windows 95 would like it to be. To do this, take the following steps:

1 Start Windows Explorer.

2 Open the Printers folder by double-clicking it.

3 Open the printer that's stalling by double-clicking it.

4 Choose the Printer Properties command.

5 Click the Details tab.

6 Set the Transmission Retry value to something big. Something really big.

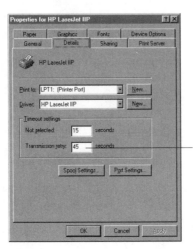

Setting the Transmission Retry value

The Transmission Retry value, in essence, tells Windows 95 how long to wait for a printer before notifying you that the printer isn't responding. For non-PostScript printers, Windows 95 assumes 45 seconds is long enough. For PostScript printers, Windows 95 assumes 90 seconds is long enough. But if you're printing graphics or printing in color, you can and should dramatically increase these settings. And I do mean dramatically. The suggested setting for a color PostScript printer, for example, is 900. Ugh.

FILES

You Want to Move a File to a Computer That's Running MS-DOS or an Earlier Version of Windows

Even though you've made the big switch—to Windows 95—you'll have friends who haven't. You know who I'm talking about, right? It'll probably be the same guy who's still got platform shoes and a lava lamp. So what happens when you want to use one of this person's **files** or when he wants to use one of yours?

Use the network

If this person is on your **network**—which is possible, I guess, although doubtful—you can share your files by saving them on a network disk drive and opening them from that drive. You can use **Windows Explorer** to do your saving and opening. Your friend can use **File Manager**.

Use a floppy disk

Hey, I've got a business idea for you. Here's what you do. Put a full-page ad in one of the big computer magazines, advertising a networking product called "Sneakernet." Tell people that for, say, $35, you'll send them everything they need to network 20 computers. Whenever anybody sends you the money, mail them a couple of boxes of disks. (It would probably be a good idea to include both 5.25-inch and 3.5-inch floppy disks.)

In all seriousness, though, you really can use **floppy disks** to move Windows 95 files to and from a computer that's running **MS-DOS**. This works because Windows 95 actually uses two names for every file: a long **file name** that you use in Windows 95 and in any Windows 95 applications and a short file name that MS-DOS and MS-DOS programs happily use.

The special new version of MS-DOS included with Windows 95 lets you display a directory list of file names that includes both the short, 8-character file name and the long file name. To do this, start MS-DOS (such as by clicking the **Start button** and then choosing Programs and MS-DOS.)

continues

You Want to Move a File to a Computer That's Running MS-DOS or an Earlier Version of Windows *(continued)*

Enter the command name *dir* to see the short and long file names of the files in a directory.

You Can't Save a File on Any Disk

Applications need a certain amount of system resources to save **files.** If these system resources get too low, you can run into some pretty serious problems. Fortunately, as long as you keep your cool, this doesn't have to be a disaster. Your basic tack is a simple one. You want to free up your system resources and then try resaving the **document.**

Close any other applications

Switch to any of the other open applications and close them. You can switch to other open applications by clicking their buttons on the **Taskbar.** Then choose from several ways to close the application. Probably the easiest way is to simply click the application window's **Close button.**

Close any documents you don't need to save

If you've opened other documents in the application that won't save some important document, you might be able to free up system resources by closing these other documents. Of course, this might present its own problem if these other documents need to be saved. In extreme cases, you might need to close the document that has the fewest unsaved changes without saving it.

The new word on system resources

The term "system resources" actually refers to special chunks of **memory**—called "local heaps"—that Windows 95 uses to store information about the applications you're running and the documents you've opened. Windows 95 still uses these local heaps, but it provides more heaps, it provides bigger heaps, and it stores far less stuff in them. For this reason, Windows 95 should have far fewer problems with low system resources than the earlier versions of Windows. And for that, we can all be thankful.

You Can't Save a File
on a Floppy Disk

If you try to save a file or copy a file on a **floppy disk** but can't, there are several things you can try.

Unprotect the floppy disk

If you get a message that says a disk is write-protected, you won't be able to save a file on, or "write to," the disk until you unprotect the disk.

To write to a 5.25-inch floppy disk, verify that the floppy disk has a notch. If a piece of tape or an adhesive tab is covering this notch, you won't be able to write anything to the disk. To unprotect the floppy disk, remove the tape or adhesive tab that covers the notch.

To write to a 3.5-inch floppy disk, verify that there is no square hole in the disk's upper right corner (when you're holding the disk so that you can read its label). If there is a square hole, flip the floppy disk over, and move the slide so that it covers the hole.

Why the write-protection

I don't mean to sound like a worrier, but before you decide it's OK to write to a previously write-protected floppy disk, you may want to consider the reasons someone protected the disk. Who knows? Maybe there's stuff on the disk that shouldn't be written over.

continues

You Can't Save a File on a Floppy Disk *(continued)*

Format the floppy disk if needed

If you get a message that a Windows-based application can't read a disk, it may be because the disk isn't formatted. If you know this is the case or if you know there's nothing on the floppy disk that you or anyone else needs, you can format the floppy disk. (For all practical purposes, formatting a disk destroys everything that's on it.)

❖ Formatting Floppy Disks

You Can't Find a File   I love large **hard disks.** It's great, just great, to have hundreds and hundreds of **megabytes** of storage. All that room makes it easy to misplace a **file,** however. Fortunately, Windows 95 provides an extremely powerful tool for finding lost files: the Find File **application.**

Because the Find File application is so powerful and so terribly useful, I'm going to describe it in detail here.

Use the Find File application

To start the Find File application, click the **Start button.** Next, choose Find and then Files Or Folders. Windows 95 displays the Find: All Files dialog box.

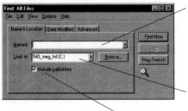

1 If you know the **file name,** type it in the Named box. You can use **wildcard characters** as part of the file name.

2 Use the Look In drop-down list box to tell Windows 95 where to look.

3 Click the Include Subfolders check box if you want to look in both the **folders** and **subfolders** of the disk you identified using the Look In box.

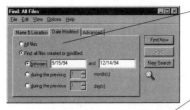

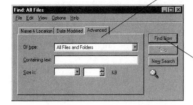

4 Optionally, use the options on the Date Modified tab to describe the last modification date of the file you're looking for.

5 Optionally, use the options on the Advanced tab to describe either some string of text that a file contains or the file size.

6 Click Find Now to start the search for the file or files you've described. When Windows 95 completes its search, it displays the Find: Files Named window, which shows a list of the files.

Multitasking is cool

If you describe a sophisticated search—say, one that looks for chunks of text in files—the search can take a long time. Perhaps hours or even days. But this doesn't have to be a problem. You can run other applications at the same time. All you need to do is start the other applications.

 Multitasking; Starting Windows-Based Applications

You Can't Open a File

If you can find a **file** but you can't open it, you've got another problem. There are several reasons why you may not be able to open a file. Most of the reasons, however, are easy to address.

Verify that the file isn't already open

It's possible that another **application** has already opened the file. If that's the case, you're not going to be able to open the same file a second time. So you'll need to first close the **document** using the application that's currently got it open. Or if you can't close the file until another application finishes whatever it's doing, you'll just have to wait.

Use an application instead of Windows Explorer

If you tell **Windows Explorer** to open a document, it first opens the application that created the document and then tells that application to open the document. But there's a potential problem. When Windows Explorer names the document that should be opened, it uses the long **file name.** If you're using an MS-DOS application or an application designed to run on top of an earlier version of Windows, however, this application will get all wigged out because it expects a short file name. It'll finally give up, telling you that it can't open a file that has a name like the one you've supplied.

Fortunately, there's an easy solution to this problem. Just use the application that created the document to open the document. You open the document in the usual way.

Opening Files

162

Your Hard Disk Is Full

If your **hard disk** begins to fill up, you'll either want to free up some space or buy a bigger disk—for two reasons. First, Windows 95 likes a certain amount of free disk space just to run because it uses **virtual memory.** Second, some Windows-based **applications** go, like, totally berserk if they encounter a full hard disk. (By "totally berserk," I just mean you'll get an application error.)

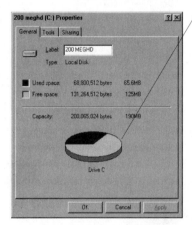

Check your free disk space by starting **Windows Explorer,** clicking the hard disk's icon, and then choosing the File Properties command. The General **tab** in the Properties dialog box includes a pie chart that shows free disk space.

Erase any unneeded files

The most direct way to free up disk space is to remove individual **files** from the disk using Windows Explorer's File Delete command. If you want to save the files, you can first copy them to a **floppy disk.**

In general, it's not a good idea to remove files you didn't create in the first place. It may be, for example, that you and Windows 95 or you and some application have different ideas about whether a file is needed.

continues

Your Hard Disk Is Full *(continued)*

Empty the Recycle Bin and reduce its size

The **Recycle Bin,** as you may know, stores deleted files. Windows 95 allocates a set percentage of your disk space—the default percentage is 10%—to use for storing the Recycle Bin's files.

The Recycle Bin is cool, no doubt. But it does use a lot of disk space. So one way to recover some disk space is to empty the Recycle Bin or to at least delete some of its files. Then, after either of these actions, you can reduce the Recycle Bin's size. To do this, follow these steps:

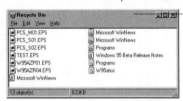

1 Display the Recycle Bin window (such as by double-clicking the Recycle Bin icon or by opening the Recycle Bin icon using Windows Explorer).

2 Choose the File Empty Recycle Bin command.

3 Choose the File Properties command.

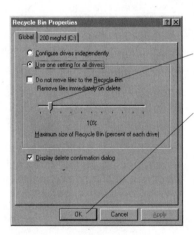

4 Move the slide control to the left so that the Recycle Bin reserves less space.

5 Click OK.

You Accidentally Erased a File

If you erase, or delete, a **file** and later realize you shouldn't have, all is not lost. As mentioned earlier, the **Recycle Bin** stores deleted files. So any recently deleted file is probably stored in the Recycle Bin. (Note that when the Recycle Bin eventually does fill up, Windows 95 makes room for newly deleted files in the Recycle Bin by removing the oldest deleted files from it. So you probably won't be able to unerase really old files using the Recycle Bin.)

Unerase the file

To unerase a file you've previously deleted, recycle the file by following these steps:

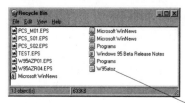

1 Display the Recycle Bin window (such as by double-clicking the Recycle Bin icon or by opening the Recycle Bin icon using **Windows Explorer**).

2 Select the file you want to unerase.

3 Choose the File Restore command.

165

QUICK
REFERENCE

Any time you explore some exotic location, you're bound to see flora and fauna you can't identify. To be sure you can identify the key commands you see in Windows 95, the Quick Reference describes these items in systematic detail.

START MENU GUIDE

Programs   Displays the Programs menu, which lists any Programs submenus as well as the MS-DOS Prompt and Windows Explorer items.

Documents   Displays a list of up to the last 15 documents you've used. To open one of the listed documents, choose the document name.

Settings   Displays the Settings submenu.

> **Control Panel** Displays the Control Panel tools as icons.

> **Printers**   Displays the Printers window so that you can add a new printer, modify an existing printer's operation, or view the documents being printed by a printer.

> **Taskbar**   Displays the Taskbar Properties dialog box so that you can change the way Windows 95's Taskbar works.

Find   Displays the Find submenu.

> **Files Or Folders** Displays the Find: All Files dialog box so that you can look for a lost file or folder.

> **Computer**   Displays the Find: Computer dialog box so that you can look for a computer on a network.

Help   Displays the Help Topics window so that you can get help with something that's bothering you— your weight, the household budget, how to use HyperTerminal, or whatever.

Run   Displays the Run dialog box, which you can use to start applications that don't appear on any Programs submenu.

Shut Down   Displays the Shut Down dialog box so that you can exit Windows 95 or suspend Windows 95 (so that it uses less power).

WINDOWS EXPLORER AND MY COMPUTER MENU GUIDE

File Menu

Open — Opens the selected folder or file. (If Windows 95 doesn't know which application opens a document, it changes the name of this command to Open With. It also prompts you for the application name when you choose the command.)

Explore — Starts Windows Explorer. (This command only appears in My Computer, of course)

Print — Prints the selected file. (Windows 95 displays this command only if it knows which application created the file.)

Quick View — Displays a picture of the file in a Quick View window so that you know what's in the file. (Windows 95 displays this command only if it knows which application created the file.)

Send To — Displays the Send To submenu, which lists the places you can move a file, such as to a floppy disk.

New — Displays the New submenu so that you can create a new folder, shortcut, or document. (The New submenu lists a handful of common documents you may want to create.)

Create Shortcut — Creates a shortcut icon for the selected file.

Delete — Erases the selected folder, program, or file.

Rename — Draws a text box around the selected folder or file so that you can change its name by typing.

Properties — Displays a dialog box you can use to display and change the properties of the selected file, folder, disk, or whatever object you've selected.

Close — Removes the active window from your screen.

169

Edit Menu

Undo   Undoes the last operation.

Cut   Removes the selected file and places it on the Clipboard so that you can paste the file someplace else.

Copy   Makes a copy of the selected file and places the copy on the Clipboard so that you can paste the file someplace else.

Paste   Moves the file currently stored on the Clipboard to the open folder.

Paste Shortcut   Creates a shortcut for the item you just copied or cut.

Select All   Selects all the files and folders displayed in the window.

Invert Selection   Selects all the unselected files and folders in the window and unselects all the selected files and folders. (If this seems just too weird, select a file and then choose the command. You'll see what happens instantly.)

View Menu

Toolbar   Displays or Hides a toolbar from the window. (Windows 95 marks the command with a checkmark when the toolbar is present.)

Status Bar   Displays or Hides a status bar from the window. (Windows 95 marks the command with a checkmark when the status bar is present.)

Large Icons   Tells Windows 95 to use big icons to represent files and folders.

Small Icons   Just as you suspected, tells Windows 95 to use tiny icons to represent files and folders.

List   Tells Windows 95 to display folders and files in a list.

Details   Tells Windows 95 to give you all the nitty-gritty details about the files it shows: name, file type, size, and date last modified.

Arrange Icons	Displays the Arrange Icons submenu.

	By Name	Arranges folders and files in alphabetical order.
	By Type	Arranges folders together and then arranges files by type. (Windows 95 uses the file extension to determine the file type.)
	By Size	Arranges files in order of increasing size.
	By Date	Arranges files in order of date last modified.
	Auto Arrange	Tells Windows 95 to tidy up in whatever way it thinks makes most sense.

Line Up Icons	Tells Windows 95 to arrange icons in neat, little rows.
Refresh	Updates the folder and file information shown in the window.
Options	Displays a dialog box you can use to control how Windows 95 lists folders and files.

About the Arrange Icons submenu commands

The Arrange Icons submenu may also list other commands that correspond to other sorting methods.

Tools Menu

Find Displays the Find submenu.

Files Or Folders Displays the Find: All Files dialog box so that you can look for a lost file or folder.

Computer Displays the Find: Computer dialog box so that you can look for a computer on a network.

Map Network Drive Connects your computer to a network disk drive.

Disconnect Net Drive Disconnects your computer from a network disk drive.

Go To Displays a dialog box that you use to name the folder you want to open.

You won't see the Tools menu everywhere...

The Tools menu appears only in windows that Windows Explorer displays. It doesn't appear in windows displayed by the Windows 95 My Computer.

Help Menu

Help Topics Displays the Help Topics dialog box.

About Windows 95 Displays the About Windows dialog box and gives information about the available memory and system resources.

PRINTERS FOLDER MENU GUIDE

File Menu

Open	Opens the selected printer so that you can see its print queue.
Pause Printing	Stops or resumes printing on the selected printer. (This command appears only if the selected printer is a local printer connected to your computer.)
Purge Print Jobs	Deletes the print jobs waiting in the selected printer's print queue. (This command appears only if the selected printer is a local printer connected to your computer.)
Set As Default	Makes the selected printer the one Windows 95 and Windows-based applications use for printing.
Sharing	Displays the Properties dialog box for the selected printer so that you can tell Windows 95 whether it should share the printer with other printers on the network.
Create Shortcut	Creates a shortcut icon for the selected file.
Delete	Removes the selected folder, program, or file.
Rename	Draws a text box around the selected folder or file so that you can change its name by typing.
Properties...	Displays a dialog box you can use to display and change the properties of the selected file, folder, disk, or whatever object you've selected.
Close	Removes the active window from your screen.

About the Edit, View, and Help menus

The Edit, View, and Help menu commands that are available when the Printers folder window is displayed are the same as the commands that are available in Windows Explorer or My Computer.

PRINTER MENU GUIDE

Printer Menu

Pause Printing	Stops or resumes printing on the selected printer.
Purge Print Jobs	Deletes the print jobs waiting in the print queue.
Set As Default	Makes the selected printer the one Windows 95 and Windows-based applications use for printing.
Properties	Displays a dialog box you can use to display and change the properties of the printer.
Close	Removes the active window from your screen.

Document Menu

Pause Printing	Stops or resumes the printing of the selected document.
Cancel Printing	Deletes the selected document from the print queue.

View Menu

Status Bar	Displays or hides a status bar in the window. (Windows 95 marks the command with a checkmark when the status bar is present.)

Help Menu

Help Topics	Displays the Help Topics dialog box.

SPECIAL CHARACTERS

... ellipsis 12, 52
* (wildcard character) 136
? (wildcard character) 136
16-bit operating system 18
32-bit operating system 18
80386 microprocessor 85
80486 microprocessor 85

A

accessibility options 52
accessories, defined 19
activating windows 19
active application. *See* foreground application
active document 20
active folder 64
active printer, changing 104
active windows
    documents vs. applications ... 19
    and foreground application 6, 19, 65
    vs. inactive windows 19
Add Printer Wizard 102-4, 153
Add/Remove Programs tool 151
Airbrush tool 98
Alt key 13, 80, 96
animation 20
ANSI characters 21
"antique" applications 21, 150-51
application errors
    defined 22
    troubleshooting 149
applications
    background vs. foreground 7, 22-23, 65
    closing when "hung" 82, 149

applications *(continued)*
    defined 21
    as files 62
    icon in Windows Explorer ... 139
    listed on Taskbar 129
    multitasking 6-7, 90, 161
    older, using 21, 150-51
    in program groups 68
    on Programs menu 5
    response problems 148-49
    sharing data between 22, 119
    starting 4-5, 94, 125
    starting automatically at
        startup 5, 127
    switching between 7, 90, 128
    terminating when "hung" 82, 149
    and threads 131
    in title bars 132
application windows
    activating 19
    active document in 20
    buttons and icons 136
    changing size 11, 43, 44, 86
    closing 39, 44
    defined 6, 22
    and foreground application 6, 65
    managing 10
    maximizing 11, 44, 86, 136
    minimizing 11, 44, 86, 136
    sharing information between 56
    shrinking to Taskbar
        buttons 11, 44, 86
Arrange Icons submenu 171
arrow keys 96
ASCII text files 22
associated documents 139
asterisk (wildcard character) ... 136
AutoPlay feature 33

B

background applications,
  defined 7, 22-23
  messages from 23
  moving to foreground 7, 65
backing up data
  to floppy disks 23-24
  restoring backed-up data 25
Backup. See Microsoft Backup
battery meter 26
bit map images, creating in Paint
  application 97-99
bit maps, defined 26
booting computer using
  MS-DOS 27
bps (bits per second) 77
Briefcase application
  adding files to briefcase 29
  creating briefcase 28
  icon 28, 140
  moving briefcase to floppy
    disk 29
  overview 28
  synchronizing briefcase
    files 29, 140
Brush tool 98
buttons. See also icons;
  option buttons
  minimized windows as 11,
    44, 86
  for window actions 136
bytes, defined 80
  See also kilobytes

C

Calculator application
  clearing inputs 31
  copying and pasting values 32
  erasing inputs 31
  inverse key 31

calculator application (continued)
  memory feature 32
  percent key 31
  starting 30
  switching to Scientific version 32
  using 30-32
Calendar application 150
canceling printing 105, 153-54
Cardfile application 150
cascading windows 54
CD Player application
  configuring 34
  overview 33
  playing music 33
CD-ROM drive 89, 140
  active application changing ... 20
  active document 20
  active printer 104
  active window 19
  date 49, 50
  desktop wallpaper 135
  object properties 122
  printer properties 104
  properties 9, 107, 122
  size of Recycle Bin 110
  time 49, 50
  time zone 49
  Windows 95 colors 40
  window size 11, 43, 44, 86
Character Map application 34-35
check boxes 12-13, 36
clicking 36
  See also right-clicking
clip art 37
Clipboard
  overview 37
  reusing contents 38
  saving contents 38
  using to copy between
    applications 119
  using to copy within
    applications 37, 46
  using to move data 87
  viewing contents 38

Clipboard Viewer
  application 38, 150
Clock application 38, 150
Close button 39, 136
Close command 44
closing
  applications 61
  dialog boxes 44
  document windows 39, 44
  documents 39
  "hung" applications 82, 149
  windows 39, 44
  Windows 95 61
colors
  changing 40
  and title bars 132
combo boxes 40
command buttons 41-42
commands
  defined 42
  overview 12-13
  using to move files 88
communications 42
  See also HyperTerminal
    application; protocols
  communications protocol 78
compound documents
  creating 94
  defined 93
  linked vs. embedded objects in ... 94
compression applications 42
CompuServe 83
connections, HyperTerminal 73-75
context menus. See shortcut menus
Control menu 43-44, 136
Control Panel 9, 45, 140
cooperative multitasking 131
copying
  data using Clipboard 37, 46
  data using drag-and-drop 56
  files in Windows Explorer 15,
    46-47
  files to another hard disk 47
  files to floppy disks 47

copying (continued)
  files using Edit Copy and Edit
    Paste commands 47
  files using File Send To
    command 46
  files using mouse 46
  multiple files 47
Ctrl key 47, 56, 80
Ctrl+Alt+Del 27, 82, 149
cursor 48
  See also selection cursor
Curve tool 99
Cut command 37, 87, 88
cutting. See moving

D

data bits 78
date, changing 49, 50
date-stamping in Notepad 92
definitions, Help 72
defragmenting disks 50-51
deleted files 3, 109
deleting
  files 60
  folders 51
  shortcut icons 122
desktop
  changing colors 40
  defined 51
  icon 139
  at startup 2-3, 124
  wallpaper for 51, 135
devices, defined 52
dialog boxes. See also wizards
  changing colors 40
  check boxes in 12-13, 36
  closing 44
  command buttons in 41-42
  list boxes in 81-82
  maximizing 44
  moving 43
  navigating with keyboard ... 13, 96

dialog boxes *(continued)*
option buttons in 96
overview 12-13, 52
selecting in 117
tabs in 13, 129
text boxes in 130
use of Alt key 13, 96
use of Tab key 96
Dial-Up Networking 111, 140
See also remote access
Direct Cable Connection 42
directories 14, 52
See also folders
disabilities, configuring
Windows 95 for 52
disk caching
read vs. write operations 53
using VCACHE 133
Disk Defragmenter application .....
50-51
disks. *See* floppy disks; hard disks
Display Properties dialog box 40
DOC file extension 63
Document menu 174
See also Documents submenu
documents
associated 139
canceling printing 105
closing 39
compound 93
creating in WordPad 142-43
deferring printing 106
defined 53
in document windows 53
as files 62
formatting in WordPad 144
list of most recently used ... 5, 54
opening automatically at
startup 5, 127
opening together with
applications 5, 95-96, 125
opening using File Open
command 95

documents *(continued)*
opening using shortcut icons ....
4, 78, 96
opening using Windows
Explorer 95, 125
pausing printing 106
printing in applications ... 105-6
printing in WordPad 144
saving before closing 39
saving in WordPad 144
saving when application is
"hung" 149
in title bars 132
types of 53
Documents submenu
cleaning up 54
list of most recently used files ... 5, 54
starting applications from ....
5, 54, 125
document windows
activating 19
active vs. inactive 19
active window 54
buttons and icons 136
cascading 54
changing size 11, 43, 44, 86
closing 39, 44
documents in 53
illustrated 10
maximizing 11, 44, 86, 136
minimizing 11, 44, 86, 136
overview 7, 54-55
shrinking to buttons .. 11, 44, 86
tiling 54
viewing all open 54
double-clicking 55, 79
DoubleSpace application 42, 55
See also DriveSpace application
downloading files 76-77
drag-and-drop technique 56
dragging 56
drawing tools 98-99
DriveSpace application .. 42, 57-58
drop-down list boxes 59, 82

E

Edit Cut command 37, 87, 88
editing in place 79
Edit menu 170, 173
Edit Paste command 37, 47, 87,
    88, 94, 119
Edit Paste Special command 37,
    94, 119
electronic mail. *See* e-mail
Ellipse tool 99
ellipsis (...) 12, 52
e-mail
    using Inbox 79
    Windows 95 support for 83
embedded objects, editing in place
    79
embedding vs. linking 94, 119
enlarging windows 11
Eraser tool 98
erasing files 59
errors, scanning for 115
exiting
    Windows 95 61
    Windows-based applications ... 61
expanding windows 11
Explorer. *See* Windows Explorer

F

F8 key 27, 124, 127
File Create Shortcut command 121
File Exit command 61
file extensions
    specifying 63
    in Windows Explorer 63
File Manager 62, 150
    See also Windows Explorer
File menu (Printers folder) 173
File menu (Windows Explorer) 169

file names
    allowable length 62
    long vs. short 63
    and older versions of
        Windows-based applications ... 63
    rules for 62
    searching for, using wildcard
        characters 136
    Windows 95 vs. MS-DOS 63
File Open command 95
file pane 15, 63, 138
File Rename command 112
files
    accidental erasures 165
    in Briefcase 28-29
    copying 46-47
    defined 14, 62
    deleted 3, 109
    deleting 60, 109, 163
    downloading using
    HyperTerminal 76-77
    and earlier Windows versions ...
        157
    listing in Windows Explorer ......
        14-15, 138
    moving 87
    naming 62-63, 114
    opening 4-5, 94-96, 125, 127
    problems opening 162
    problems saving 158-60
    README files 108
    recovering 109, 165
    in Recycle Bin .. 3, 109-10, 164-65
    renaming 112, 114
    resaving 114
    saving 113-14
    searching for 160-61
    selecting in Windows Explorer
        139
    troubleshooting 157-65
    undeleting 109, 165
    uploading using HyperTerminal
        77
    viewing with Quick View 108

File Save As command 62-63, 113, 114

File Save command........... 113, 114

file transfer protocols ... 76, 77, 145

Fill With Color tool 98

Find File application 160-61

finding

    files 136, 160-61

    Help topics 71

Find submenu 168, 172

flashing Taskbar buttons 23

flashing title bar 23

floppy disks

    and Briefcase files 28-29

    copying files to 46

    displayed in My Computer 8

    formatting 66, 160

    overview 64

    problems saving files 159-60

    sizes of 64

    and Sneakernet 157

    write protecting 159

folder icon (Windows Explorer) ... 139

folder pane 14, 64, 138

folders

    active 64

    animation use 20

    creating in Windows Explorer ... 64

    defined 14, 64

    deleting 51

    within folders 64

    viewing in Windows Explorer ... 14-15, 64, 138

fonts

    adding 133

    overview 65

    point size 101

    PostScript 102

    TrueType 132-33

    in Windows Explorer 65, 140

    in WordPad application 144

foreground application, defined 6, 65

foreground window.

    See active windows

Format dialog box 66

formatting floppy disks 66, 160

Free Cell game 67

Free-Form Select tool 98

G

games, uses for 67

gigabytes, defined 67

glossary, Help 72

groups, program 68

H

hard disks

    compressing data 42, 57

    copying files to 47

    defined 68

    defragmenting 50-51

    making room on 163-64

    maximum capacity in

      Windows 95 67

    uncompressing 57

    viewing in Windows Explorer ... 139

Hearts game 67

Help glossary 72

Help menu 13, 69, 172, 173, 174

Help, online 69-72

Help shortcut buttons 70, 120

Help table of contents 69-70

hourglass pointer 70, 101

HyperTerminal application

    communications protocol 78

    connecting to another

      computer 75

HyperTerminal application (continued)

describing connections 73-74
disconnecting from another
computer 78
downloading files 76-77
overview 42, 72
saving connection descriptions
.... 75
uploading files 77

I

icons. See also buttons;
shortcut icons
for opening documents 4, 78, 96
overview 8, 78
in Windows Explorer 15, 139-40
inactive applications.
See background applications
inactive windows 10, 19
Inbox 79
increasing window size ... 11, 43, 44, 86
INI file extension 111
initialization files 111
in-place editing 79
insertion point 48, 79, 97
Insert Object command 94
Ins key 97
installing new applications 151
Intel microprocessors 85
international settings.
See regional settings
Internet 80, 83

K

keyboard
scrolling with 117
shortcut keys 13, 80
kilobytes, defined 80

L

languages. See regional settings
laptop computers
battery meter 26
and Briefcase application 28-29
checking battery level 26
deferring printing 106
dial-up access to desktop
computer 111
exchanging files with desktop
computers 28-29, 82, 111
local access to desktop
computer 42, 82
Windows 95 features 81
Line tool 99
linking vs. embedding 94, 119
list boxes 13, 81-82
local connections 82
local heaps 159
local reboot 82
LOG file extension 92
logging on 3, 83
long file names 63

M

Magnifier tool 98
mail. See e-mail
Maximize button 86, 136
maximizing windows ... 11, 44, 86, 136
Media Player application 83
megabytes, defined 84
memory 67, 84
See also virtual memory
menu bars 12, 84
menu guide 169-72
as shell 120
menus
example 85
keyboard shortcuts for
commands 80

menus *(continued)*
overview 12-13
message boxes, defined 85
microprocessors 85
Microsoft Backup application ... 23-25
Microsoft Network 83, 86
Microsoft Windows 95.
   See Windows 95
Minesweeper game 67
Minimize button 136
minimizing
   application and document
      windows 11, 44, 86, 136
   restoring to previous size 11,
      43, 86, 136
modems. *See also* Phone Dialer
      application
   defined 87
   need for 72, 86
mouse
   clicking 36
   dragging to move files 87
   honing skills with games 67
   left vs. right buttons 112-13
   right-clicking 112-13, 122
   scrolling with 116
   selecting with 117
mouse pointers, defined 101
Move command 43
moving
   data using Clipboard 37, 87
   data using drag-and-drop 56
   dialog boxes 43
   files by dragging mouse 87
   files to another folder 87-88
   files using menu commands 88
   files using Windows Explorer
      87-88
   Taskbar 129
   windows 11, 43
MS-DOS
   as 16-bit operating system 18
   directories 14
   and F8 key 27, 124, 127

MS-DOS *(continued)*
   file names 63
   getting command prompt 89
   moving Windows 95 files to 157
   running applications 27, 88
   starting 27, 61, 124
   and virtual machines 27, 88, 133
   when to use 27
MS-DOS Prompt command 89
MSN. *See* Microsoft Network
multimedia
   overview 89
   playing files 83
   plug and play 101
multitasking. *See also* threads
   overview 6-7, 90, 161
   preemptive vs. cooperative 131
   switching between applications
      .... 7, 90, 128
music. *See* CD Player application
My Briefcase icon 28, 140
My Computer
   defined 90
   as graphical map 8
   icon 2, 139

naming files 62-63, 114
Net communications. *See*
   HyperTerminal application
Network Neighborhood
   defined 91
   as graphical map 8, 9
   icon 2, 140
networks. *See also*
   Microsoft Network
   defined 91
   logging on 3, 83
   for moving files to other
      computers 157
   sending e-mail 83
Notepad application 91-92

N

O

objects
    changing properties 122
    defined 93
    embedded 79
    linked vs. embedded 94
OLE 93-94
online communications. *See*
    HyperTerminal application
online Help 13
online services 83
opening files
    applications 4-5, 94, 125
    documents ... 4, 5, 78, 95-96, 125
    options for 94-96
    from shortcut icons 4, 78, 96
    from Start button 4, 94, 124
    at startup 5, 127
    troubleshooting 162
    from Windows Explorer 94,
    95, 128
operating systems
    16-bit vs. 32-bit 18
    MS-DOS vs. Windows 95 18
option buttons 96
overtyping 97

P

pages, dialog box. *See* tabs, in
    dialog boxes
Paint application
    creating bit map images ... 97-99
    list of tools 98-99
Paintbrush application 100, 150
    See also Paint application
panes, window 137
    See also file pane; folder pane
parity 78
Party Line game 67

passwords
    assigning to screen savers 116
    for logging on 3, 83
Paste command 37, 47, 87,
    88, 94, 119
Paste Special command 37, 94, 119
patterns, desktop 51
pausing printing 106, 154
peer-to-peer networks 91, 141
Pencil tool 98
Pentium microprocessor 85
permanent swapfile 134
PgDn key 117
PgUp key 117
Phone Dialer application 100
phone numbers
    in HyperTerminal application
    73-74
    in Phone Dialer application ... 100
Pick Color tool 98
PIF files 100, 133
plug and play, defined 101
pointers, defined 101
point size 101, 132
Polygon tool 99
pop-up boxes 72, 101
postponing printing 106, 154
PostScript 102
power usage 128
preemptive multitasking 131
Printer menu 174
printers
    adding with Add Printer Wizard
    .... 102-4, 153
    changing properties 104
    changing which is active 104
    describing 102-4
    displayed in My Computer 8
    stalling of 156
    transmission retry setting 156
    troubleshooting 152-53
Printers folder 8, 173

printing
  bit map images 99
  canceling 105, 153-54
  deferring 106
  overview 105
  pausing 154
  retrying 155-56
  troubleshooting 152-56
  viewing print queue 105
Print Manager 105
  See also Printers folder
print queue 105-6
print spool files 105, 154
program groups 68
program items 106
Program Manager 21, 68, 106,
  120, 150
  See also Windows Explorer
programs. *See* applications
Programs menu 5, 94, 125, 126
properties, changing 9, 107, 122
property sheets 107
protocols, defined 107
  See also communications
  protocol; file transfer protocols

question mark (wildcard character)
  136
queue. *See* print queue
Quick View feature 108

radio buttons. *See* option buttons
README files 108
rebooting computer 82
receiving downloaded files ... 76-77
Recorded Rectangle tool 99
recovering erased files 165
Rectangle tool 99

Recycle Bin
  changing size of 110, 164
  emptying 109, 164
  icon 78, 140
  overview 3, 109
  turning off feature 110
  undeleting files 109
reducing window size 11, 43, 44, 86
regional settings 110-11
registry 111
remote access 42, 111, 140
renaming
  files 112, 114
  shortcut icons 122
resaving files 114
resizing
  Taskbar 129
  windows 11, 43
Restore button 136
restoring
  backed-up data 25
  window size 11, 43, 86, 136
right-clicking 112-13, 122
root directory 113

saving
  bit map images 99
  documents when application is
  "hung" 149
  files 113-14
  troubleshooting 158-60
scalable font technologies
  PostScript 102
  TrueType 132-33
ScanDisk application 115
Scientific Calculator 32
screen savers 115-16
scroll bars 11, 116, 117
  See also slide controls
scrolling 117

Q

R

S

searching
    for files 160-61
    using wildcard characters 136
selecting
    defined 117
    multiple list items 81
    noncontiguous list items 81
    single list items 81
selection cursor 48, 117
Select tool 98
Settings submenu 168
shapes, drawing 99
sharing data 22, 119, 157
shell 106, 120
    See also My Computer
Shift key 47
shortcut buttons (Help) 70
shortcut icons
    adding to menus 126
    creating 121
    deleting 122
    for older Windows-based
      applications 151
    opening files with 4, 78, 96
    overview 4, 78, 120-21
    renaming 122
    uses for 122
shortcut menus 122
short file names 63
shrinking windows 11, 44, 86
Shut Down command 61, 128
Size command 43
slide controls 123
    See also scroll bars
SmartDrive application 123
Sneakernet 157
software programs. *See* applications
Solitaire game 67
sound files 123
Sound Recorder application 123
special characters, adding to
    documents 34-35
splitting windows into panes ... 137
spool files 105, 154

Start button
    starting applications from 4,
      94, 124
    using in multitasking 128
starting
    applications 4-5, 94, 125
    MS-DOS 27, 61, 124
    older Windows-based
      applications 21, 150-51
    Windows 95 .... 2, 124
Start menu
    adding shortcut icons to ... 126, 151
    list of commands 168
    overview 4, 125
Startup menu 5, 127
    See also Windows 95 Startup
    menu
startup options 124, 127
stop bits 78
subfolders 14, 127, 138
submenus 5, 127
Suspend option 128
swapfile 134
switching tasks 7, 128
symbols, adding to documents
    34-35
SYSTEM.INI file 111
system resources 159
System Tools folder 9

T

Tab key 96
tabs, in dialog boxes 13, 129
Taskbar
    battery meter on 26
    buttons on 23, 129
    defined 7, 129
    minimized applications on ... 11,
      44, 86
    moving 129
    resizing 129
    Start button 124, 128, 129

Taskbar buttons, flashing 23
task buttons 129
tasks, switching 128
telecommunications. *See*
    HyperTerminal application
telephone dialer. *See* Phone dialer
    application
telephone numbers
    in HyperTerminal 73-74
    in Phone Dialer application ... 100
Terminal application 130, 150
    See also HyperTerminal application
terminating "hung" application
    .... 82, 149
text boxes 12-13, 130
text editing in WordPad 143
text editor. *See* Notepad application
text files 22
Text tool 99
threads 131
tiling windows 54
time
    changing 49, 50
    displaying 38
time-stamping in Notepad 92
time zone, changing 49
title bars
    defined 10, 132
    flashing 23
toolbars 132
Tools menu 172
trackball pointers 101
Transmission Retry value 156
troubleshooting
    application response 148-49
    file problems 157-65
    finding files 160-61
    floppy disk problems 159-60
    full hard disk 163
    opening files 162
    printing 152-56
TrueType fonts 132-33

TXT file extension 92
    unassociated documents 140
    unminimizing windows 86
    uploading files 77

V

VCACHE application 53, 133
View Details command 15
View menu 170-71, 173, 174
virtual machines 27, 88, 133
virtual memory 134, 163
viruses 134

W

wallpaper, desktop 51, 135
wildcard characters 136, 160
window buttons 136
window panes 137
windows
    activating 19
    active vs. inactive 10, 19
    application vs. document ... 6-7,
        10, 19
    background vs. foreground ... 19
    buttons and icons 136
    cascading 54
    changing colors 40
    changing size 11, 43, 44, 86
    closing 39, 44
    maximizing 11, 44, 86, 136
    minimizing 11, 44, 86, 136
    moving 11, 43
    restoring 11, 43, 86, 136
    shrinking to buttons 11, 86
    splitting into panes 137
    switching among 20
    tiling 54

Windows 95
    as 32-bit operating system 18
    closing 61
    desktop 2-3
    exiting 61
    logging on 3, 83
    maximum hard disk size 67
    maximum memory capacity ... 67
    and networks 91
    online Help 69-72
    starting 124, 127
    system tools 8-9
Windows, earlier versions
    limitations of 141
    transferring files to 157
    using applications from 21,
    150-51
Windows Explorer
    checking disk space 163
    copying files 46-47
    creating shortcut icons 121
    erasing files 60
    file extensions 63
    file pane 63, 138
    folder pane 64, 138
    formatting floppy disks 66
    icons 15, 139-40
    menu guide 169-72
    moving files 87-88
    opening files from 94, 95, 125
    overview 14-15, 138
    previewing fonts 65
    Quick View feature 108
    renaming files 112
    selecting disks 138
    selecting files 139
    selecting folders 138
    starting 138
    starting applications from 21,
    94, 150-51
Windows for Workgroups 141
Windows NT 18, 141

Windows 95 Startup menu 27,
    124, 127
Windows Taskbar. *See* Taskbar
Wingdings characters 34
WIN.INI file 111
wizards
    Add Printer Wizard 102-4, 153
    defined 142
WordPad application
    creating documents 142-43
    editing text 143
    saving documents 144
    using fonts 144
    vs. word processors 145
word wrapping 145
Write application 21, 145
    See also WordPad application
XLS file extension 63

Z

Zmodem protocol 76, 77, 145

The manuscript for this book was prepared and submitted to Microsoft Press in electronic form. Text files were prepared using Microsoft Word 6.0 for Windows. Pages were composed by Stephen L. Nelson, Inc., using PageMaker 5.0 for Windows, with text in Minion and display type in Copperplate. Composed pages were delivered to the printer as electronic prepress files.

COVER DESIGNER
Rebecca Geisler-Johnson

COVER ILLUSTRATOR
Eldon Doty

INTERIOR TEXT DESIGNER
The Understanding Business

PAGE LAYOUT AND TYPOGRAPHY
Stefan Knorr

COPY EDITOR
Barbara Browne

TECHNICAL EDITOR
Scott Thompson

INDEXER
Julie Kawabata

Printed on recycled paper stock.

WHO KNOWS MORE
ABOUT WINDOWS® 95
THAN
MICROSOFT® PRESS?

ISBN 1-55615-816-5
224 pages
$19.95 ($26.95 Canada)

ISBN 1-55615-683-9
320 pages
$29.95 ($39.95 Canada)

These books are essential if you are a newcomer to Microsoft®
Windows® or an upgrader wanting to capitalize on your knowledge
of Windows 3.1. Both are written in a straightforward, no-nonsense
way, with well-illustrated step-by-step examples, and both include
practice files on disk. Learn to use Microsoft's newest operating
environment quickly and easily with MICROSOFT WINDOWS 95 STEP
BY STEP and UPGRADING TO MICROSOFT WINDOWS 95 STEP BY STEP,
both from Microsoft Press.

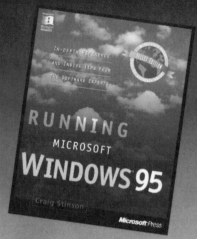